MW00939336

Bible Study Guide

Joshua

Good Questions Have
Small Groups Talking

By Josh Hunt

© Copyright 2015 Josh Hunt
If you enjoy this, you might check out the hundreds of lessons
available at a low subscription price at
http://mybiblestudylessons.com/

All scripture quotations, unless otherwise indicated, are taken
from the Holy Bible, New International Version®, NIV®. Copyright
©1973, 1978, 1984, 2011 by Biblica, Inc.™ Used by permission
of Zondervan. All rights reserved worldwide. www.zondervan.
com The "NIV" and "New International Version" are trademarks
registered in the United States Patent and Trademark Office by
Biblica, Inc.™

Contents

Joshua, Lesson #1
Good Questions Have Small Groups Talking

www.joshhunt.com

You might invite your people to watch this video series in preparation for today's lesson: https://www.youtube.com/playlist?list=PLZmR8vK7kkQCxoqZ8pIEZjNseyW4wGgze (Or search YouTube for Forgotten Chapters of the Old Testament, Josh Hunt)

Joshua 1.1 - 9

OPEN
Let's each share your name and, what is one favorite Bible verse?

DIG
1. Context. About what year is this?

> Many know the stories of the Old Testament; they do not know the story. When I teach in the Old Testament, I like to set the context.

2. If you have a smart phone, find a picture of the Jordan River.

http://en.wikipedia.org/wiki/Jordan_River

3. How do you imagine they felt they neared the Jordan?

Joshua and Israel have just one. In literal terms it is not very impressive. For much of the year the Jordan as it draws near the Dead Sea is a shallow, muddy affair. But symbolically, it is a big deal. On the other side of it are all those Canaanites, whose large size struck the Israelite spies a generation ago (see Numbers 13–14). Historically, they are indeed a much stronger and more sophisticated people than the Israelites. Two and a half of Israel's twelve clans have looked at the country east of the Jordan where Israel is camped at the moment ("across the Jordan" from the perspective of the people telling the story later). They have spotted that it is rather good and have asked that they might settle there. One can imagine that the other nine-and-ahalf clans might be wondering whether there is room for them there, too. Yet the real promised land lies west of the Jordan. There is a river to cross. — John Goldingay, *Joshua, Judges, and Ruth for Everyone: A Theological Commentary on the Bible, Old Testament for Everyone* (Louisville, KY; London: Westminster John Knox Press; Society for Promoting Christian Knowledge, 2011), 8–9.

4. What does the name "Joshua" mean?

Moses was dead. A representative, a picture, a type of the Law, Moses brought the people to the edge of the Promised Land, but it would be Joshua, whose name is the Old Testament name for Jesus, who would actually bring them in to the Promised Land.

In Numbers 13:8, we read that Joshua's name was originally Hoshea. Hoshea means "salvation." Joshua was indeed saved when the blood was applied to the house of Nun during the Passover. As firstborn, he would have died otherwise. So his name, "Salvation," was an appropriate one. But Moses changed his name from Hoshea to Joshua, from "Salvation" to "Jehovah is Salvation," signifying that Jehovah alone brings salvation. — Jon Courson, *Jon Courson's Application Commentary: Volume One: Genesis–Job* (Nashville, TN: Thomas Nelson, 2005), 638.

5. What would you say is the theme of this section?

No fewer than four times we read that they were to be strong, courageous, confident, fearless (vv. 6, 7, 9, 18). In fact, the ninth verse comes right out and says, "Do not tremble or be dismayed." Today we would say, "Don't get stressed out. Don't let intimidation do a number on you."

Anytime (yes, any time) there is a new furrow to be plowed, a new path to be cleared, a new idea to be tried, or a new strategy to be implemented, fear of failure stands as tall as a giant. And all too often, it pushes its way in and gains a foothold. It has been my observation that the greater the possibility of impact, the greater the fear of failure ahead of time. That is what makes the Canaan invasion so exciting. It was so incredible, so humanly impossible, it had all the makings of a classic, Guinness Book of World Records failure.

How often we Christians unknowingly tip our hands. We pray with beseeching hands lifted high, "Oh, Lord, almighty and omnipotent God, who knows no barrier and who cannot fail, we present this need to you today in prayer." And then immediately on the heels of that theologically powerful petition, we frown as we look around the table and say, "Gentlemen, the situation we face today is completely hopeless . . . nothing can be done." When will we ever learn that there are no hopeless situations, only people who have grown hopeless about them? What appears as an unsolvable problem to us is actually a rather exhilarating challenge. People who inspire others are those who see invisible bridges at the end of dead-end streets.

There was a Cabinet meeting in London during the darkest days of the Second World War. France had just capitulated. Prime Minister Churchill outlined the situation in its starkest colors. Quite literally, the tiny British Isles stood alone. Grim faces stared back at him in stoic silence. Despair and thoughts of surrender were written in their looks. The visionary statesman momentarily remained silent, lit a cigar, showed a hint of a smile, and with a twinkle in his eye, responded to that dispirited company of officials, "Gentlemen, I find it rather inspiring." He was the one who, on another occasion, said, "Nothing in life is so exhilarating as to be shot at without result." What a great line! No wonder people followed the man. Fear of failure never entered his mind. — Charles R. Swindoll, *Dropping Your Guard* (Nashville: Thomas Nelson, 2009).

6. Why was it important that they be strong and courageous?

An entire fighting force—a mighty army—moving ahead without fear of failure. By faith, they moved out.

Everyone who starts a new venture—whether a Charles Lindbergh carefully planning to cross the Atlantic, a Henry Ford launching an infant industry into the mainstream of world transportation, or a homemaker deciding to go back to school or start a business—faces certain fears, inner struggles, and temptations to quit. But there are ways of planning and of handling adversity and setbacks which have often made the difference between those who have risked and succeeded and those who have never really begun.

Those are the words of a man who literally turned garbage into a multimillion-dollar business mainly because he refused to be intimidated by the fear of failure.

As I think about those ancient Hebrews and the magnificent way God assimilated and mobilized them into a secure fighting force, I realize a third principle was put into operation. — Charles R. Swindoll, *Dropping Your Guard* (Nashville: Thomas Nelson, 2009).

7. Why is it important that we live lives that are strong and courageous?

Fear, it seems, has taken a hundred-year lease on the building next door and set up shop. Oversize and rude, fear is unwilling to share the heart with happiness. Happiness complies and leaves. Do you ever see the two together? Can one be happy and afraid at the same time? Clear thinking and afraid? Confident and afraid? Merciful and afraid? No. Fear is the big bully in the high school hallway: brash, loud, and unproductive. For all the noise fear makes and room it takes, fear does little good.

Fear never wrote a symphony or poem, negotiated a peace treaty, or cured a disease. Fear never pulled a family out of poverty or a country out of bigotry. Fear never saved a marriage or a business. Courage did that. Faith did that. People who refused to consult or cower to their timidities did that. But fear itself? Fear herds us into a prison and slams the doors.

Wouldn't it be great to walk out? — Max Lucado, *Fearless: Imagine Your Life without Fear* (Nashville: Thomas Nelson, 2009).

8. How does fear harm us?

Fear does this. Fear corrodes our confidence in God's goodness. We begin to wonder if love lives in heaven. If God can sleep in our storms, if his eyes stay shut when our eyes grow wide, if he permits storms after we get on his boat, does he care? Fear unleashes a swarm of doubts, anger-stirring doubts.

And it turns us into control freaks. "Do something about the storm!" is the implicit demand of the question. "Fix it or . . . or . . . or else!" Fear, at its center, is a perceived loss of control. When life spins wildly, we grab for a component of life we can manage: our diet, the tidiness of a house, the armrest of a plane, or, in many cases, people. The more insecure we feel, the meaner we become. We growl and bare our fangs. Why? Because we are bad? In part. But also because we feel cornered.

Martin Niemöller documents an extreme example of this. He was a German pastor who took a heroic stand against Adolf Hitler. When he first met the dictator in 1933, Niemöller stood at the back of the room and listened. Later, when his wife asked him what he'd learned, he said, "I discovered that Herr Hitler is a terribly frightened man." Fear releases the tyrant within. — Max Lucado, *Fearless: Imagine Your Life without Fear* (Nashville: Thomas Nelson, 2009).

9. **Can you think of other places in the Bible where we are told to not be afraid?**

His most common command emerges from the "fear not" genre. The Gospels list some 125 Christ-issued imperatives. Of these, 21 urge us to "not be afraid" or "not fear" or "have courage" or "take heart" or "be of good cheer." The second most common command, to love God and neighbor, appears on only eight occasions. If quantity is any indicator, Jesus takes our fears seriously. The one statement he made more than any other was this: don't be afraid.

Siblings sometimes chuckle at or complain about the most common command of their parents. They remember how Mom was always saying, "Be home on time," or, "Did you clean your room?" Dad had his favorite directives too. "Keep your chin up." "Work hard." I wonder if the disciples ever reflected on the most-often-repeated phrases of Christ. If so, they would have noted, "He was always calling us to courage."

So don't be afraid. You are worth much more than many sparrows. (Matt. 10:31 NCV)

Take courage, son; your sins are forgiven. (Matt. 9:2 NASB)

I tell you not to worry about everyday life—whether you have enough. (Matt. 6:25 NLT)

Don't be afraid. Just believe, and your daughter will be well. (Luke 8:50 NCV)

Take courage. I am here! (Matt. 14:27 NLT)

Do not fear those who kill the body but cannot kill the soul. (Matt. 10:28)

Do not fear, little flock, for it is your Father's good pleasure to give you the kingdom. (Luke 12:32)

Don't let your hearts be troubled. Trust in God, and trust also in me. . . . I will come and get you, so that you will always be with me where I am. (John 14:1, 3 NLT)

Don't be troubled or afraid. (John 14:27 NLT)

"Why are you frightened?" he asked. "Why are your hearts filled with doubt?" (Luke 24:38 NLT)

You will hear of wars and rumors of wars, but see to it that you are not alarmed. (Matt. 24:6 NIV)

Jesus came and touched them and said, "Arise, and do not be afraid." (Matt. 17:7)

Max Lucado, Fearless: Imagine Your Life without Fear (Nashville: Thomas Nelson, 2009).

10. What does fear feel like? Describe a time when you were afraid.

And fear feels dreadful. It sucks the life out of the soul, curls us into an embryonic state, and drains us dry of contentment.

We become abandoned barns, rickety and tilting from the winds, a place where humanity used to eat, thrive, and find warmth. No longer. When fear shapes our lives, safety becomes our god. When safety becomes our god, we worship the risk-free life. Can the safety lover do anything great? Can the risk-averse accomplish noble deeds? For God? For others? No. The fear-filled cannot love deeply. Love is risky. They cannot give to the poor. Benevolence has no guarantee of return. The fear-filled cannot dream wildly. What if their dreams sputter and fall from the sky? The worship of safety emasculates greatness. No wonder Jesus wages such a war against fear. — Max Lucado, *Fearless: Imagine Your Life without Fear* (Nashville: Thomas Nelson, 2009).

11. How? How do we overcome fear? How do we, "be strong and courageous"?

Christ followers who overcome fear successfully have learned that when they face their fears, God does His part. He shows up, and His presence is tangible. He is a more than adequate partner for the journey. And He has filled Scripture with words of truth that can keep your fears at bay.

The psalmist David experienced debilitating fears at times, and he found God to be a faithful Deliverer: "I sought the LORD, and he answered me; he delivered me from all my fears."[62]

Joshua, who had the unenviable task of following in Moses' footsteps and leading the Israelites into the Promised Land, received this message from God: "As I was with Moses, so I will be with you; I will never leave you nor forsake you. . . . Have I not commanded you? Be strong and courageous. Do not be afraid; do not be discouraged, for the LORD your God will be with you wherever you go."[63]

God can be counted on to show up and do His part. He will be with you when you face your fear. Speaking words of truth from His promises is key to conquering what you are afraid of. The art of speaking truthfully with words of Scripture is a skill that can be strengthened with practice. Over time it will become second nature, and it will be a powerful weapon in your arsenal against fear. — Bill Hybels, *Simplify: Ten Practices to Unclutter Your Soul* (Carol Stream, IL: Tyndale, 2014).

12. What good things comes to the strong and courageous?

Over and over again, God tells Joshua, "Be strong and courageous. Be strong and courageous. Be strong and courageous. Be strong and very courageous. Don't be afraid." Strength and courage should typify us, characterize us, define us. Because of the Spirit that's inside of us, we should not be afraid.

Some days I feel discouraged, even defeated. My church friends sometimes slip their arm around me, cry with me, and say things like,

"I'm so sorry. I know it's tough."

"Why don't you take a vacation?"

"Maybe you need more family time."

"You should get more sleep."

I'm longing for the day when someone instead says to me, "Francis, you know what? You're a powerful person. The Holy Spirit of God is inside you. I know things are difficult. But be strong and courageous."

I don't know many believers who gather together and encourage each other to be strong. Peter and John astonished people with their boldness, and yet when they got out of jail, they prayed for more boldness! In Ephesians 6:19 — 20, Paul, the boldest guy on earth, says, "Pray for me, that I can preach the word boldly." The body of Christ needs once again to lay hands on each other, praying for boldness and strength. We should remind each other that we serve an almighty God. He's coming back, and every knee will bow. He swore to himself that it's going to happen. We may look stupid now, but we need to stay on his side and do everything his Word says. Let's live it. Let's walk it. Let's urge each other on toward boldness, power, strength. The church of Jesus Christ should once again be known as strong, bold, and courageous. — Craig Groeschel, *What Is God Really Like? Expanded Edition* (Grand Rapids, MI: Zondervan, 2010).

13. Joshua 1.8 has three steps to life-changing Bible study. Can you find all three?

Imagine a chef who collected cookbooks, took cooking classes, studied recipes, and developed menus—but never cooked. Are you like that when it comes to spiritual food? It's one thing to enjoy Bible study, attend Bible classes, and follow daily reading plans. But are you daily applying the Bible's lessons to your attitudes and behavior?

Joshua 1:8 gives three steps to Bible study. First, keep listening to God's Word. Keep reading it aloud. Don't let it depart from your mouth or your mind.

Second, meditate on it. Mull it over in your imagination. Think about it when you drive to work and when you sit at home. Ponder it when you lie down and when you rise up.

Third, obey it—be careful to do everything in it. Then you will make your way prosperous, and then you will have good success. When we're consistent in our daily devotions, it's easier to be consistent in our daily duties. — David Jeremiah, *Turning Points with God: 365 Daily Devotions* (Carol Stream, IL: Tyndale, 2014).

14. Compare Joshua 1.8 with Psalm 1. What do they have in common?

That is how it is with the man in Psalm 1. He does not determine his course of action by what those without God say—even in their latest brilliant ideas. That is, he does not live as if God does not exist, nor does he make plans from within a strictly human understanding. He "does not walk in the counsel of the wicked" but in the counsel of God (verse 1).

The Psalm 1 man delights in the law of God (see verse 2). He loves God's law, is thrilled by it, and can't keep his mind off of it. He thinks it is beautiful, strong, wise, and an incredible gift of God's mercy and grace. He therefore dwells upon it day and night, turning it over and over in his mind and speaking it to himself.

The result is a flourishing life. The image used here is that of a tree planted by water canals. No matter what the weather or the surface condition of the ground, its roots go down into the water sources and bring up life. As a result, it bears fruit when it is supposed to, and its foliage is always bright with life. It prospers in what it does. The same is true for the man who is rooted in God through his law: "In whatever he does, he prospers" (verse 3; compare Joshua 1:8). — Dallas Willard and Don Simpson, *Revolution of Character: Discovering Christ's Pattern for Spiritual Transformation* (Colorado Springs, CO: NavPress, 2005), 160.

15. Verse 8. What does it mean to meditate? How do we meditate?

The phrase "meditate on his law day and night" may sound intimidating, unrealistic, or undesirable. How would I ever get any work done if I spent the whole day contemplating Lamentations? But that's not necessary. That is not the idea.

There is an old saying that if you can worry, you can meditate. Meditating is simply turning a thought over and over in your mind. As you do that, neurons are firing and your brain is rewiring. When you receive information that matters to you, you can't help meditating on it.

When I was in high school, a friend of mine told me about a girl who liked me. I could not believe it, because I knew this girl and she was way out of my league.

"This can't be true," I said.

"But it is true," my friend said. "I don't understand it either, but it's true."

That night my mind fixated on this thought: She likes me. I couldn't stop thinking about it. My mind just went there over and over. She likes me. So the next day, although I could hardly believe it was true, I called her up and asked her out.

It turned out it wasn't true.

But I had one really good night thinking about it. It was my delight, and what I delight in, I can't help thinking about.

What would it look like to delight in the law of the Lord? It certainly is something deeper than being thrilled about a bunch of rules in the Bible. It starts with a vision of being loved by God. God is way out of my league. He is in the perfection league; I am in the fallen league. This wonderful God, this mysterious, all-powerful, all-holy God — he loves me! Periodically this truth bursts in, and we can't stop thinking about it. — John Ortberg, *The Me I Want to Be* (Grand Rapids, MI: Zondervan, 2010).

16. How are scripture memory and meditation related?

The most obvious thing we can do is draw certain key portions of Scripture into our mind and make them a part of the permanent fixtures there. This is the primary discipline for the thought life. We need to know these passages like the back of our hand, and a good way to do that is to memorize them and then constantly turn them over in our mind as we go through the circumstances of our daily life (see Joshua 1:8; Psalm 1).

We cannot realize the desired effect by focusing on isolated verses, but it will certainly come as we ingest passages, such as Romans 5:1–8; 8:1–15; 1 Corinthians 13; or Colossians 3:1–17. When you take these into your mind, your mind will become filled with the light of God himself.

You may say, "I can't memorize like that." I assure you, you can. God made your mind for it, and he will help you. He really wants you to do this. As you choose to give your time and energy to the transformation of your mind, it will happen! You will discover that the mind of the Spirit is life and peace, and in every deflection of life, your mind will automatically recenter on God as the needle of a compass returns to north. — Dallas Willard and Don Simpson, Revolution of Character: Discovering Christ's Pattern for Spiritual Transformation (Colorado Springs, CO: NavPress, 2005), 94.

17. How can scripture memory and meditation help us to deal with fear?

I love the way Brennan Manning describes this journey to inner wholeness: "Genuine self-acceptance is not derived from the power of positive thinking, mind games, or pop psychology. It is an act of faith in the grace of God alone."[2]

Ultimately I cannot make fear go away with positive thinking, mind games, or pop psychology. Only faith in the One who knows me and knows the path toward fullness can take me to the place of freedom I so desperately long for.

That is also why I love the sacred words that God shared with Joshua. It is exactly what I feel like Jesus is saying to me each time he brings me to a new manifestation of the intersection of faith and fear:

> Have I not commanded you? Be strong and courageous. Do not be afraid; do not be discouraged, for the LORD your God will be with you wherever you go. (Josh. 1:9)

God knew Joshua's particular boundary of fear and invited him to cross it. If Joshua had chosen fear, he would have chosen a life with restrictions and boundaries. But to choose faith was to choose a life that crossed over those fear-induced boundaries. It was a life of walking with God, a life of adventure and intimacy, mystery and excitement.

When the writer of Hebrews tells us to fix our eyes on Jesus, the author and pioneer of faith, he is inviting us to live in the exact same way. — Daniel Hill, John Ortberg, and Nancy Ortberg, *10:10: Life to the Fullest* (Grand Rapids, MI: Baker, 2014).

18. What good things can we expect as we meditate on God's Word?

Maybe Joshua was still wavering. Maybe he wasn't quite sure he wanted the job of leader. (And maybe you can relate!) Whatever Joshua was thinking, God told him again, for the second time, "Be strong and very courageous" (Joshua 1:7). In essence, God coached his tentative handpicked leader, "Take even more courage, Joshua!"

Why, Lord?

"Because I have given you the battle plans that will guide you to success! And now I'm giving you all the strength you will need to pull it off, to make it happen."

God gave Joshua guidance, and He gives it to you, too, through His Word. So, as God cautioned Joshua, "do according to all the law which Moses My servant commanded you" (verse 7).

This reminds me of a story I heard of a championship football team that was defeated by a weaker team. It didn't matter what play was run—the opponent seemed to know exactly how to defend against the play. The coaches on the stronger team were baffled as they tried to make sense of their loss. Then, sometime later, the mystery was solved: The opposing team had somehow obtained one of their team's playbooks. The stolen playbook gave the opposing team a guide to victory. They knew every play the other team might possibly attempt.

God has given you a playbook as well—the Bible. This means you can make a strong, successful defense against fear and the flaming missiles of the evil one (Ephesians 6:16). So purpose to follow God's advice to Joshua. Don't get distracted and lose your courage. Don't turn to the right or to the left. Keep your devotion focused on God and His playbook for your life. "Then you will have good success...wherever you go" (Joshua 1:8-9). — Jim George, *A Leader after God's Own Heart: 15 Ways to Lead with Strength* (Eugene, OR: Harvest House, 2012).

19. What do you want to recall from today's conversation?

20. How can we support one another in prayer this week?

I found this video of the Jordan River at flood stage. https://www.youtube.com/watch?v=quDZ298uF4E You might email your group and ask them to take a look.

Joshua 3

OPEN

Let's each share your name and what is the biggest risk you have ever taken?

DIG

1. Read this passage for application. What is the lesson for us?

It's a nice image, "getting your feet wet." I think its background lies in this story. Often you can't achieve something or experience something or learn something without making a commitment that may seem risky. It would be nicer to have proof that things will be okay before you make the commitment, but life does not work that way. If you give in to commitment anxiety, you live without danger, but also without life. Ever since we first saw people hang gliding in the French Alps, my very short list of things I wanted to do before I die included "Go hang gliding." Eventually with a friend I drove into the foothills of the mountains northeast of where I live to an airstrip where we left our car to be driven along the steep and narrow unfenced track up the side of a mountain to its flatish top (I remember reflecting that I was more likely to die by the van careering off this track than by hang gliding). I got strapped in behind an experienced glider, and we ran to the edge of a cliff and jumped off. To realize your ambitions, at some point you have to jump off, or jump in. — John Goldingay, *Joshua, Judges, and Ruth for Everyone: A Theological Commentary on the Bible, Old Testament for Everyone* (Louisville, KY; London: Westminster John Knox Press; Society for Promoting Christian Knowledge, 2011), 15–16.

2. Verses 1, 2. Why do you suppose God had them camp there for three days?

God told the people of Israel to wait three days at shores of the Jordan River (Joshua 1:11). All that time, the people of Israel saw a rushing river, swollen with spring rains laying in front of them. They must have asked, "How can we ever cross this river?"

i. It was one thing for a few spies to make their way across (as happened in Joshua 2), but here we are talking about a nation of millions, with all their possessions—how will they make it?

b. At a moment like this, all the wonderful talk about living in the Promised Land can sound pretty hollow. There is a seemingly impossible obstacle blocking the way—how will God do this one? — David Guzik, *Joshua, David Guzik's Commentaries on the Bible* (Santa Barbara, CA: David Guzik, 2000), Joshua 3:1, 2.

3. Imagine this as scene in a movie. How do you picture it?

Joshua had hundreds of thousands of fighting men, so the number gathered on the banks of the Jordan could not have been fewer than two million. (Forty thousand armed men prepared for war from the tribes of Reuben, Gad and half the tribe of Manasseh crossed over with all the others, 4:13.) The crowds must have stretched for miles along the river! The wonder is that they gathered there without murmuring or questioning. We don't read of any dissent. But to attempt the crossing would mean certain death, and they knew it. How could mothers and babies, pregnant women and children, sheep and cattle cross the swollen, one-and-a-half-kilometre-wide river (for 'the Jordan overflows all its banks during the whole time of harvest', 3:15)? Yet they gathered in expectancy and faith. The crossing would need to be accomplished in the daylight hours of a single day. They did not know how it would be accomplished, but they knew that their God would not leave them stranded on the east side of the river. This was a massive act of faith in the face of impossible circumstances. — Colin N. Peckham, *Joshua: A Devotional Commentary, Exploring the Bible Commentary* (Leominster, UK: Day One Publications, 2007), 83.

4. What do we learn about faith from this story?

Joshua had told the people, (chap. 1:11.) that they were to pass over Jordan. But it doth not appear that they were informed how. Reader! it is good to have faith exercised. Abraham was not told that a ram would be provided when the Lord led him to the mount of sacrifice. Moses had no consciousness that the Lord would dry the Red Sea until the hour of need. The sinner little thinks, when first the Lord begins a work of grace in his heart, that deliverance shall come, and in a way so astonishing as the blood and righteousness of Jesus? Doth not our God say to us upon numberless occasions, as to the poor man in the gospel, Believest thou that I am able to do this? Matt. 9:28. — Robert Hawker, *Poor Man's Old Testament Commentary: Deuteronomy–2 Samuel, vol. 2* (Bellingham, WA: Logos Bible Software, 2013), 189.

5. Verse 1. Why do you suppose Joshua got up early?

Joshua was an early riser (6:12; 7:16; 8:10), who spent the first hours of the day in communion with God (1:8). In this, he was like Moses (Ex. 24:4; 34:4), David (Ps. 57:8; see 119:147), Hezekiah (2 Chron. 29:20), and our Lord Jesus Christ (Mark 1:35; see Isa. 50:4). It's impossible to live by faith and ignore the Word of God and prayer (Acts 6:4); for faith is nurtured by worship and the Word. The people God uses and blesses know how to discipline their bodies so that they can give themselves to the Lord in the early morning hours. — Warren W. Wiersbe, *Be Strong, "Be" Commentary Series* (Wheaton, IL: Victor Books, 1996), 45–46.

6. Verse 3. What was the Ark? How big was it? What did it represent?

Crossing the Jordan is tied to the preparation period by chronological references. Joshua arose early in the morning and moved the camp from Shittim to the river. After three days, Joshua's officers walk through the camp giving final instructions on the order for crossing the Jordan. The operation plans order the people to wait for the signal to move. When priests pick up the ark of the covenant, the symbol of the presence of God, and begin the march, the people then follow at least two thousand cubits behind the ark. (A cubit is about eighteen inches or half a meter.) The ark will guide the march through the river for possessing the land.

Marching behind the ark reinforces the theological belief that God as supreme commander leads Israel. Only the Lord knows the future and can guide the people to victory in the land of Canaan. The people remain a half-mile behind the ark in respect of the power of God, because the Lord is holy, and that holiness is dangerous. At every point the people depend on God, for they do not know the way to victory. The journey to Canaan depends on God's showing them the way. — J. Gordon Harris, "Joshua," in Joshua, Judges, Ruth, ed. W. Ward Gasque, Robert L. Hubbard Jr., and Robert K. Johnston, *Understanding the Bible Commentary Series* (Grand Rapids, MI: Baker Books, 2012), 32.

7. Circle every occurrence of the word "ark" in this narrative.

No longer did the pillar of fire lead them. They were now led by the ark, which represented the presence of God. The ark was a box made of shittim or acacia wood and covered with gold; it was 1.5 cubits broad (0.7 metre), 1.5 cubits high and 2.5 cubits long (1.1 metres). It is known as the 'ark', the 'ark of the covenant' or the 'ark of Testimony'. It was to be carried by the priests to the middle of the river and held there until all the Israelites had passed over the Jordan. The people had to maintain a respectful distance of 2000 cubits (about 900 metres) from the ark. It could not be treated casually. This would also prevent crowding around the ark, keeping it in full view of all the people all the time. The ark dominated the crossing:

- the ark to be seen (3:3);

- the ark at the brink of the Jordan (3:6);

- the ark to be borne by priests (3:8);

- the ark into the Jordan (3:11);

- the ark in the Jordan—waters cut off (3:13);

- the ark in the Jordan, ahead of the people (3:14);

- the ark borne by priests on dry ground in the Jordan (3:17);

- the ark in the Jordan—waters cut off (4:7);

- the ark in the Jordan—twelve stones set up to mark the feet of the priests (4:9);

- the ark carried across after the people (4:11);

- the ark comes out of the Jordan (4:16);

- the ark out of the Jordan—waters return (4:18).

Every development and event is linked to the ark. This is not Joshua's crossing or war; God was in control and he was leading them into a conflict that would destroy the Canaanites and all their vile iniquity. — Colin N. Peckham, *Joshua: A Devotional Commentary, Exploring the Bible Commentary* (Leominster, UK: Day One Publications, 2007), 84–85.

8. **Verse 4. How long is a cubit? Why were they required to stay back?**

God required that they keep some 1,000 yards behind the ark. This was for two reasons. First, to respect the holy nature of the ark of the covenant. But also, it was to make sure that everyone a clear view of the ark. That you may know the way by which you must go shows that the ark of the covenant led the way. Israel would accomplish this impossible task as they set their eyes upon God's presence, and followed only after His presence. — David Guzik, *Joshua, David Guzik's Commentaries on the Bible* (Santa Barbara, CA: David Guzik, 2000), Jos 3:3–5.

9. **Verse 5. The Old King James had, "sanctify yourselves." What does sanctify mean?**

The word "sanctify" is quodosh in Hebrew. It means "to set apart" or "to prepare." If you filled a glass full of rocks and then attempted to pour a pitcher of water into it, the amount of water that could be poured in would be limited by the rocks in the glass. If you really wanted more water in the glass, the key wouldn't be to keep pouring more water because it would just spill out. The key would be to remove the rocks.

The same thing is true spiritually. A lot of people are trying to be filled with the Spirit when in reality they need to be emptied of sin. They need to say, "Search my heart, Lord. Show me the things that are restricting the flow of Your Spirit. Show me the rocks." — Jon Courson, *Jon Courson's Application Commentary: Volume One: Genesis–Job* (Nashville, TN: Thomas Nelson, 2005), 646–647.

10. **It is always a good idea to read the Bible for emotion. What do you think it felt like for them on this day?**

As the nation waited by the Jordan River, the people must have wondered what Joshua planned to do. He certainly wouldn't ask them to swim the river or ford it, because the river was at flood stage (3:15). They couldn't construct enough boats or rafts to transport more than a million people over the water to the other side. Besides, that approach would make them perfect targets for their enemies. What would their new leader do? — Warren W. Wiersbe, *Be Strong, "Be" Commentary Series* (Wheaton, IL: Victor Books, 1996), 45.

11. Verse 13. Why do you suppose God didn't part the waters before they got there? What is the lesson for us?

When the priests and representatives from each tribe put their feet into the river, the water would divide. Forty years previously, when the children of Israel crossed the Red Sea, the water parted before they stepped in (Exodus 14). But not this time. When it comes to the issues of the Spirit, we're to step in by faith.

"But what if hands are laid upon me and I seek the Lord's power aggressively, yet nothing happens? I'll feel like a big drip," we say. So we stay on the bank where it's safe and dry—real dry, dusty dry, wilderness dry.

Why doesn't God part the water first? I'm convinced it's because the language of eternity is faith. This life is only eighty years long at best. So God uses every opportunity to teach us to see and hear with the eyes and ears of faith. "Step out. Step in. Step up in faith," He says. "And watch and see what I'll do." — Jon Courson, *Jon Courson's Application Commentary: Volume One: Genesis–Job* (Nashville, TN: Thomas Nelson, 2005), 647.

12. Verse 13. Exactly when did the waters part? Again, what is the lesson for us?

You can learn a lot sitting in traffic.

Imagine side-by-side left-hand turn lanes. One lane has three cars waiting to turn left, while the other has 20. The people in the longer line want to make sure that they will be able to make their next turn after the light. The people in the shorter line, on the other hand, want to make it through the light faster and will worry about making their next turn later. The long-line people and the short-line people have different tolerances for risk—or perhaps different levels of faith.

No matter which person you are in this situation, faith is often spelled R-I-S-K. When the priests carried the Ark into the Jordan River at flood stage, there was a risk they could lose the Ark to the Jordan River. However, that is not what happened. "And as soon as the priests who carry the ark of the LORD—the Lord of all the earth—set foot in the Jordan, its waters flowing downstream will be cut off and stand up in a heap" (Joshua 3:13). God changed the entire environment and made it possible to walk across the Jordan without the pressure of wading through the powerful water—but only after they took the first step.

Risk means there is a potential for loss. However, when God leads us to take a risk, He is there with us whether we succeed or fail—He is there in the success and He is there in the failure. If He leads you to take a risk, you may not always succeed in the way you think. In fact, you may even fail.

The only true failure, though, is when we fail to take the risks God is leading us to. Sometimes, the fear of failure is the greater obstacle than the risk itself.

Has God called you to step out in an area that requires risk? This could be the place He wants you to move. Ask Jesus to give you the courage to step out. — Os Hillman, *TGIF: Today God Is First* (Grand Rapids, MI: Baker, 2011).

13. Verse 15. Why didn't God just arrange for this crossing at some other time of year?

'Then he brought us out from there, that he might bring us in, to give us the land of which he swore to our fathers' (Deuteronomy 6:23). This was the objective. Now the Israelites stood before the flooded river Jordan with the immediate prospect of entering the land.

God would cause the river to dry up for several reasons:

- It would enable an immediate and easy entry into the land.

- It would facilitate instant military occupation.

- It would reveal his power to a new generation. The God who could dry up the Red Sea was the same God who would dry up the Jordan. The new generation would witness the power of God over nature.

- Joshua's position would be confirmed, because he predicted the event and it came to pass. He would be seen obviously to be God's chosen successor to Moses.

- The awesome spectacle of a nation crossing the river would cause the inhabitants of Canaan to be devastated psychologically. They would have felt secure because the flooded river formed a natural barrier to any hostile force, but once the hordes poured over the dry riverbed, 'their heart melted; and there was no spirit in them any longer' (5:1). — Colin N. Peckham, *Joshua: A Devotional Commentary, Exploring the Bible Commentary* (Leominster, UK: Day One Publications, 2007), 82.

14. What did it feel like to be Joshua on this day? What do we learn about following God from this?

Imagine that your family is in desperate trouble. You are facing financial obstacles so gigantic there is no way you are going to survive economically. You may lose your home, your business, and your reputation. In fact, you are in such deep trouble that your greatest fear is that you might lose your family.

And then...God speaks to you directly—in an audible voice! He tells you that He is going to exalt you in the presence of your whole family. He is going to work a great miracle—and you will be the one to lead your family out of the deep crisis. God next reveals that as a result of delivering your family, everyone who sees the miracle happen will consider you a great hero.

God then says that you are to tell your family what He has just revealed to you. How would you react? Obviously, you would consider sharing everything God told you—including the statement that He was going to exalt you! After all, that is what God said. And you were supposed to tell your family what God said!

Now, multiply this fantasy a thousand times, substituting the name "Joshua" for yours and think in terms of "your family" being all the children of Israel. However, don't consider it a fantasy but a reality.

In this chapter we're going to see what Joshua did when confronted with an opportunity to exalt himself based on a direct message from God. His response is impressive. — Gene A. Getz and Frank Minirth, *Men of Character: Joshua* (Nashville: B&H, 1995).

15. What was the lesson God was teaching His people through this event?

Israel is facing an obstacle, a barrier, a particularly terrifying Plan B. They've got to get across the Jordan to get to God's life for them. And God has promised that his power is sufficient to make that happen. God will deliver them. God will make a way.

But (and this is a big but) they have to take the first step. They will not see God's power, they will not experience his faithfulness, until they get their feet wet.

God tells them, "I want you to take one step in the Jordan, and then you'll see me at work." He's teaching his people how that trust works.

And here's what happens:

When the priests carrying the Ark came to the edge of the river and stepped into the water, the water upstream stopped flowing. It stood up in a heap a great distance away. (Josh. 3:15–16)

See, God is teaching his people: I have so much power, and I want to manifest it in your life. But if you want to see my power, you have to take the risk. You have to take the step. You have to take the spiritual risk of trusting me first.

He's teaching us too. We have to take that risk if we're going to live the kind of lives God has called us to live, to be the people God dreamed of when he thought us into existence. So many miss out on this designed life because we make an unconscious vow that we will only trust ourselves and the things we think we can control.

You see, this isn't really about Joshua. It's not about Will. It's about you.

What's your Jordan River? What is your Plan B situation? Where is God asking you to take a seemingly impossible step, a step of faith?

Because here's what I know: everybody faces a Jordan. Every one of us faces a barrier that is keeping us from the life God has for us. — Pete Wilson, *Plan B: What Do You Do When God Doesn't Show up the Way You Thought He Would?* (Nashville: Thomas Nelson, 2010).

16. Is following God risky?

Retreat or risk? Throughout redemptive history, that question has confronted God's people. As John Piper references in the pages ahead, it was the decision facing the Israelites on a crucial day at Kadesh Barnea. Standing on the brink of the Promised Land, with the guarantee of God within their grasp, they ran from risk and chose to retreat. Instead of staking their lives on the faithfulness of God, they recoiled in fear. The cost was great, and the Lord left an entire generation to waste away in a wilderness until they died.

THE COMMISSION IS CLEAR

Fast-forward a few thousand years, and you come to the people of God standing in a similar moment. We live in a world where half the population is living on less than two dollars a day, and over a billion people dwell in desperate poverty. Such physical need is only surpassed by spiritual poverty. Billions of people are engrossed in the worship of false gods, and approximately two billion of those people are still unreached with the gospel, meaning that they have little chance of even hearing about the sacrifice of Christ for their sins before they die. Most of the unreached live in hard-to-reach areas of the world that are hostile to Christians—areas of the world where our brothers and sisters are presently being persecuted, imprisoned, and killed.

Though the challenges facing the church are great, the commission Christ has given is clear: make disciples of all the nations. Spend your lives spreading the gospel of God for the glory of God to the ends of the earth. As you go, trust in his sovereign authority, depend on his indwelling presence, and experience his incomparable joy. — David Platt, "Foreword," *in Risk Is Right: Better to Lose Your Life than to Waste It* (Wheaton, IL: Crossway, 2013), 7–8.

17. When have you taken a risk in following God? Who has a story?

In life, there are no safe places or risk-free activities. Helen Keller, author, speaker, and advocate for disabled persons, asserted, "Security is mostly a superstition. It does not exist in nature, nor do the children of men as a whole experience it. Avoiding danger is no safer in the long run than outright exposure. Life is either a daring adventure or nothing."

Everything in life brings risk. It's true that you risk failure if you try something bold because you might miss it. But you also risk failure if you stand still and don't try anything new. G. K. Chesterton wrote, "I do not believe in a fate that falls on men however they act; but I do believe in a fate that falls on them unless they act." The less you venture out, the greater your risk of failure. Ironically, the more you risk failure—and actually fail—the greater your chances of success. — *Failing Forward*

ARE YOU WILLING TO TAKE A RISK—EVEN FAIL— TO HAVE A DARING ADVENTURE?

— John C. Maxwell, *The Maxwell Daily Reader: 365 Days of Insight to Develop the Leader within You and Influence Those around You* (Nashville: Thomas Nelson, 2008).

18. What does failure to risk cost us?

From an early age, we are encouraged by friends, relatives, and those who care about us to "be careful," "take it easy," and "watch out." The thinking behind these admonitions is that we've got to avoid dangerous situations and eliminate risk in our lives. It is certainly prudent to avoid exposing ourselves to unnecessary danger; however, the idea of eliminating risk is counterproductive. Risk is all around us. It invades every area of our personal and professional lives. There is a false assumption that one choice carries risk with it while the alternative choice is risk free.

In the investment world, the riskiest investments are considered to be real estate and the stock market, while guaranteed bank or government accounts are considered the safest investments. While the bank and government investments do guarantee that you will not lose your money, over the last fifty years they have proven to be the most dangerous and risk-laden decisions you could have made.

While the stock market and real estate invariably go up and down, at times reminiscent of a roller coaster, over the long haul they have consistently performed well and offered good investment returns. On the other hand, over the same half-century, the "safe and conservative" investments, which are guaranteed by banks or the government, have not even kept up with inflation; therefore, they inevitably lose value.

Prudent financial advisers will tell you that there is a place for all kinds of investments. I would certainly agree; however, the point we want to understand is that risk and safety rarely are easily identified and totally pure.

I know people who are afraid to fly, so they drive on cross-country trips. Their fear, obviously, is that they could be a victim of a plane crash if they fly on an airplane. While this is statistically possible, the risk of dying in a plane crash is insignificant compared to the risk of driving your own vehicle. In reality, more people are injured or killed driving to the airport than on a commercial airliner.

Every successful business began adrift in a sea of risk. There were a multitude of things that could go wrong for every one that could go right. Many start-up ventures fail, but a few grow, prosper, and eventually succeed. The only way to guarantee failure in a business venture is never to begin. If you launch your dream, you might fail. If you never start, you are guaranteed to fail.

As you go through your day today, reexamine risk and safety. Never take a risk you don't have to, but never play it safe when it guarantees your failure. — Jim Stovall, *Today's the Day* (Colorado Springs, CO: David C Cook, 2010).

19. Summary. What do we learn about following God from this story?

Like Moses before him, Joshua received his orders from the Lord, and he obeyed them by faith. "So then faith comes by hearing, and hearing by the word of God" (Rom. 10:17, NKJV). It has been well said that faith is not believing in spite of evidence but obeying in spite of consequence. When you read Hebrews 11, the great "faith chapter" of Scripture, you discover that the people mentioned there all did something because they believed God. Their faith wasn't a passive feeling; it was an active force. Because Abraham believed God, he left Ur and headed for Canaan. Because Moses believed God, he defied the gods of Egypt and led the Jews to freedom. Because Gideon believed God, he led a small band of Jews to defeat the huge Midianite army. Living faith always leads to action. "For as the body without the spirit is dead, so faith without works is dead also" (James 2:26, NKJV). — Warren W. Wiersbe, *Be Strong, "Be" Commentary Series* (Wheaton, IL: Victor Books, 1996), 45.

20. How can we support one another in prayer this week?

Joshua, Lesson #3
Good Questions Have Small Groups Talking
www.joshhunt.com

There are some interesting videos on YouTube about Jericho. Email your people and have them to a search for "Jericho archeology" on YouTube.

Joshua 6

OPEN

Let's each share your name and what is the biggest risk you have ever taken?

DIG

1. **Anyone get a chance to look at some videos about Jericho on YouTube? What did you learn?**

2. **There is an old song that goes, "Joshua fit the battle of Jericho." As we read, try to figure out what is wrong with the theology of that song.**

   Here is Joshua with the original marching band, blowing literal horns (made from ram's horns and made for noise, not metal trumpets (they appear in Israel only later). "Joshua fit the battle of Jericho" goes a song I didn't hear one of these bands play, but Joshua didn't fight. There was no battle at Jericho. If anyone fought at Jericho, as at the Reed Sea, it was not the Israelites but God. The Israelites simply process, blow horns, and shout loudly. While there is indeed a procession by a marching band, the essential involvement of the priests makes it more like the procession around the parish bounds that churches sometimes do. The presence of the covenant chest signifies God's presence. When the Israelites made their ill-fated attempt to conquer Canaan under their own steam, there was a link between their failure and their not taking the chest with them (Numbers 14:44). Yet on a later occasion they took it with them on another ill-fated expedition, and this didn't work (1 Samuel 4). If the project is God's, the chest as the symbol of their covenant relationship with God will be an effective sign of God's presence. — John Goldingay, *Joshua, Judges, and Ruth for Everyone: A Theological Commentary on the Bible, Old Testament for Everyone* (Louisville, KY; London: Westminster John Knox Press; Society for Promoting Christian Knowledge, 2011), 27.

3. **You will need a Study Bible for this one. How big was Jericho? Anyone have a Study Bible with a note?**

Jericho was a city of about 9 acres that would have taken about 20–30 minutes to march around. This unusual battle plan would require great faith and would be another lesson in walking by faith, not by sight (Jer. 17:5–8; Heb. 11; 12). As in the crossing of the Jordan, the prominence of the ark would remind Israel that this was the work of their God. The trumpet blast is also symbolic of the presence of God—cf. Ex. 19:13; Ps. 24:7; Is. 18:3; 1 Cor. 15:52; 1 Thess. 4:16; Rev. 11:15. — W. A. Criswell et al., eds., *Believer's Study Bible, electronic ed.* (Nashville: Thomas Nelson, 1991), Jos 6:2.

4. **Why do you think God had them walk around the city? What was God trying to teach them?**

As His people marched around the walls of Jericho, God prepared them in several ways. First, He gave them a realization of the impossibility of their situation. The first time the Israelites circled the city, the walls must have looked huge. And they must have looked bigger and more foreboding with each successive trip. Thus, in their repeated journeys around the Jericho, the Lord was showing His people that victory would not come through their might nor through their power, but only by His Spirit (Zechariah 4:6).

Right now there might be a huge wall between you and a family member, neighbor or fellow believer. God will have you go around it again and again until you finally say, "I can't manipulate the situation. I can't solve the problem. I can't do a thing about this, Lord. Only You can solve this." And when at last you come to this realization, I promise you that in due season, He will do something earth-shattering. Oh, it might take six months or even six years—but there will come a time when you'll say, "It was the Lord who brought that wall down. It wasn't my cleverness or my ingenuity because as I went in circles day after week after month, it just go thicker and higher." — Jon Courson, *Jon Courson's Application Commentary: Volume One: Genesis–Job* (Nashville, TN: Thomas Nelson, 2005), 654–655.

5. Why seven days?

Secondly, as His people circled the walls of Jericho, God taught them the importance of patience. Hebrews 6:12 says that it is through faith and patience that His promises are obtained. Do you have faith? Great. God wants you to have patience, too. You see, His agenda is bigger than just knocking down walls. His purpose is to develop patience in us in order that we might be perfect, lacking nothing (James 1:4). — Jon Courson, *Jon Courson's Application Commentary: Volume One: Genesis–Job* (Nashville, TN: Thomas Nelson, 2005), 655.

6. Circle every occurrence of the word "seven" in this passage.

On that basis, the command is given: "You shall march around the city ..." (v. 3), and all the subsequent instructions then follow. For each of the next six days the whole army is to march around the city walls once. But the emphasis is not on the fighting men but on the ark of the covenant, the symbol of the divine presence. God is with his people, in their very midst, to accomplish his victory for them. He is not remote or at arm's length but is leading his people by his presence, just as he had done through all their wilderness years. That is why there is such an emphasis on the number "seven" in the text, occurring four times in just one verse (v. 4). Seven is the number of divine perfection or completeness, reflecting the seventh day of rest at the end of the six days of creation. So here the six days circling the city are to find their completion or culmination in the seventh day with its seven circuits around Jericho. The presence of the ark is heralded by seven priests each with a ram's horn trumpet, blown "continually" (v. 9), culminating in a long blast after the seventh circuit on the seventh day, which is the sign for a great shout from the people and the collapse of the city walls. The ESV footnote draws our attention to the literal translation both in verse 5 and verse 20: "the wall of the city will fall under itself"; that is, it will collapse as though from pressure from above rather than from outside. — David Jackman, *Joshua: People of God's Purpose, ed. R. Kent Hughes, Preaching the Word* (Wheaton, IL: Crossway, 2014), 69.

7. What do you think would have happened if the people of Jericho would have repented during these seven days?

As Israel marched and played the rams' horns, what if the people of Jericho had run out on day seven and said, "Please don't destroy us; have mercy on us; we repent of our sins and we believe in your God!"? Would God have relented? He did for Rahab, and he did for Nineveh, and he would have for Sodom and Gomorrah. We have every reason to believe that he would have done the same for Jericho. We read in 2 Peter 3:9, "The Lord is not slow in keeping his promise, as some understand slowness. He is patient with you, not wanting anyone to perish, but everyone to come to repentance." So the "perfect melody" of seven horns for seven days accompanied by marching feet and a great shout could have been a call to repentance—never answered by the people of Jericho.

How many times has God marched around us waiting for us to repent and seek his forgiveness and mercy? He is patient with us, but eventually the seventh day comes. Teachers often give a "grace period" for finishing a paper or project, but eventually it has to be dealt with. God employed his marching tactic so Israel would have a chance for faith and perhaps so the Canaanites would have a chance for mercy. — *Holman Old Testament Commentary – Joshua.*

8. Verse 2. Note the tense of the verb. What was the lesson for them? What is the lesson for us?

The promise of the Lord (Josh 6:2). It's possible that the Lord spoke these words to Joshua when He confronted him at Jericho (5:13–15). The tense of the verb is important: "I have given Jericho into your hand" (6:2, NKJV, italics added). The victory had already been won! All Joshua and his people had to do was claim the promise and obey the Lord.

Victorious Christians are people who know the promises of God, because they spend time meditating on God's Word (1:8); they believe the promises of God, because the Word of God generates faith in their hearts (Rom. 10:17); and they reckon on these promises and obey what God tells them to do. To "reckon" means to count as true in your life what God says about you in His Word.

"Be of good cheer," Jesus told His disciples; "I have overcome the world" (John 16:33). "And they that are Christ's have crucified the flesh with the affections and lusts" (Gal. 5:24). "Now is the judgment of this world; now shall the prince of this world be cast out" (John 12:31). Christ has conquered the world, the flesh, and the devil; and if we reckon on this truth, we can conquer through Him. It's possible to believe a promise and still not reckon on it and obey the Lord. Believing a promise is like accepting a check, but reckoning is like endorsing the check and cashing it. — Warren W. Wiersbe, *Be Strong, "Be" Commentary Series* (Wheaton, IL: Victor Books, 1996), 71.

9. Verse 10. Why do you think God had them keep quiet as they walked?

Thirdly, as His people circled the walls of Jericho, God taught them discipline. His job was to work, theirs to be absolutely silent. If I can't control my tongue, I won't conquer the enemy. My tongue will get me in big trouble. So will yours (James 3:5, 6). Therefore, it is the wise man or woman who silently—without complaint or opinion—gives God time and room to work.

God's strategy for conquering Jericho served not only to prepare the children of Israel but to provide a witness to the people of Jericho. I believe that the people walking in quietness and tranquility, the ark of the covenant, the trumpets playing were all to be a witness to the inhabitants of Jericho. According to Rahab, their hearts were already melted. Thus, I believe God was giving them one last opportunity to come to Him. While His people were in Egypt, God gave the inhabitants of Canaan four hundred years to repent. Then He gave them forty more years while His people wandered in the wilderness. Here, He gives them six more days as they watched His children walk in devotion and order.

What will impress around you? Seeing you walk patiently and quietly, neither panicking nor complaining, but simply walking under the authority of your Captain. Seeing the way your homes, marriages, and lives are ordered in this march towards heaven is a witness to the people of our own Jerichos. — Jon Courson, *Jon Courson's Application Commentary: Volume One: Genesis–Job* (Nashville, TN: Thomas Nelson, 2005), 655.

10. **Verse 4. Just for fun, let's all make trumpets with a piece of paper. On three, I want you all to blow your trumpets! Let's try to imagine what this sounded like.**

Here is Joshua with the original marching band, blowing literal horns (made from ram's horns and made for noise, not melody), not metal trumpets (they appear in Israel only later). "Joshua fit the battle of Jericho" goes a song I didn't hear one of these bands play, but Joshua didn't fight. There was no battle at Jericho. If anyone fought at Jericho, as at the Reed Sea, it was not the Israelites but God. The Israelites simply process, blow horns, and shout loudly. While there is indeed a procession by a marching band, the essential involvement of the priests makes it more like the procession around the parish bounds that churches sometimes do. The presence of the covenant chest signifies God's presence. When the Israelites made their ill-fated attempt to conquer Canaan under their own steam, there was a link between their failure and their not taking the chest with them (Numbers 14:44). Yet on a later occasion they took it with them on another ill-fated expedition, and this didn't work (1 Samuel 4). If the project is God's, the chest as the symbol of their covenant relationship with God will be an effective sign of God's presence. — John Goldingay, *Joshua, Judges, and Ruth for Everyone: A Theological Commentary on the Bible, Old Testament for Everyone* (Louisville, KY; London: Westminster John Knox Press; Society for Promoting Christian Knowledge, 2011), 27.

11. How do you suppose there were feeling at around day five?

A clear strategy. First an armed guard marching ahead of the priests, then seven priests with seven trumpets, then the ark and the rear guard following the ark. Trumpets playing all the time but no speaking whatsoever. What was the purpose of all this? Clearly to test Israel's faith and to show that the battle was in God's hands. God sent a message to his people. These ram's horns called them to worship, not to war, and the ark in the middle of all the activity indicated God's presence. This became God's battle in every way. And remember, the walls didn't crack a little more each day to give them encouragement. Even on day seven after seven times around, nothing had yet happened. They seemed no closer to bringing down those walls than when they started. The second day they did the same thing, and the text sums up the rest of the first six days by a simple sentence: They did this for six days (v. 14).

Every day they received their instructions; every day God tested their faith. Marching again? In silence except for the seven trumpets? What will this prove? What's Joshua waiting for? What if they come over the walls and attack us? The whole scene has an ominous mystery about it. The text does not tell us whether the activity threw greater fear into the inhabitants of Jericho or whether they relaxed their defenses and went back to business as usual. In any case, it didn't make any difference—the outcome had been predetermined.

They had to march by faith, play trumpets by faith, walk out each day by faith, and then eventually shout a victory cry by faith. Hebrews 11:30 tells us, "By faith the walls of Jericho fell, after the people had marched around them for seven days." The first battle in the promised land was a battle for faith.

We all have Jericho walls that stand in the way of our spiritual victory. Anger, bitterness, lust, fear, unforgiveness, selfishness, pride, materialism, and indifference, to name a few. Paul reminds us in 2 Corinthians 10:3-4: "For though we live in the world, we do not wage war as the world does. The weapons we fight with are not the weapons of the world. On the contrary, they have divine power to demolish strongholds." — *Holman Old Testament Commentary – Joshua.*

12. What was their key to success?

"Joshua did not take the city merely by a clever, human military tactic," wrote Francis A. Schaeffer. "The strategy was the Lord's."

No situation is too great for the Lord to handle, and no problem is too much for Him to solve. When He saw more than 5,000 hungry people before Him, Jesus asked Philip, "Where shall we buy bread, that these may eat?" Then John adds, "But this He said to test him; for He Himself knew what He would do" (John 6:5–6, NKJV). God always knows what He will do. Our responsibility is to wait for Him to tell us all that we need to know and then obey it.

At the close of the last chapter, I quoted J. Hudson Taylor's words about three different ways to serve the Lord: (1) to make the best plans we can and hope they succeed; (2) to make our own plans and ask God to bless them; or (3) to ask God for His plans and then do what He tells us to do. Joshua received his orders from the Lord, and that's why Israel succeeded.

God's plan for the conquest of Jericho was seemingly foolish, but it worked. God's wisdom is far above ours (Isa. 55:8–9) and He delights in using people and plans that seem foolish to the world (1 Cor. 1:26–29). Whether it's Joshua with trumpets, Gideon with torches and pitchers (Jud. 7), or David with his sling (1 Sam. 17), God delights in using weakness and seeming foolishness to defeat His enemies and glorify His name. "For the eyes of the Lord run to and fro throughout the whole earth, to shew Himself strong in the behalf of them whose heart is perfect toward Him" (2 Chron. 16:9). — Warren W. Wiersbe, *Be Strong, "Be" Commentary Series* (Wheaton, IL: Victor Books, 1996), 71–72.

13. Verses 6, 11. What was the significance of the Ark?

The ark was especially mentioned and meticulously positioned. Joshua 'had the ark of the LORD circle the city' (v. 11). That was the issue. The important thing was not only that they compassed the city, but that the ark compassed the city, and that they were with it on its journey. The ark, of course, represented the presence of God and the person of the Lord Jesus. This symbolizes the victory we have through the presence of God, and, in particular, through the person of the Lord Jesus himself. It was God's battle and he was in the midst of his people. — Colin N. Peckham, *Joshua: A Devotional Commentary, Exploring the Bible Commentary* (Leominster, UK: Day One Publications, 2007), 108.

14. Review: tell me what you know about the Ark of the Covenant.

15. What chance did the people of Jericho have?

Those in Jericho could have recognized the danger which threatened them by the armed men who led the procession. They could have realized the certainty of an Israelite victory which was set before them by the trumpet-blowing priests.

These men were making no pretence of celebrating a victory that had not yet occurred. They should have feared when they saw the ark of the covenant itself. They knew of the Red Sea crossing, the victories in the wilderness, and the parting of the Jordan River. This covenant-keeping God was before them for evaluation. They did wrong by keeping their gates closed to him. The patience of a long-suffering God had been displayed. The seventh day brought intensified warnings, but they did not heed those warnings and judgement fell. — Colin N. Peckham, *Joshua: A Devotional Commentary, Exploring the Bible Commentary* (Leominster, UK: Day One Publications, 2007), 109.

16. Why did God place this enemy in their path? What is the lesson for us?

Christians who come through the wilderness into the land of full salvation discover to their amazement that, immediately, Jericho confronts them. To many this is incomprehensible. They expected to be overflowing with joy and glory, having trusted God when they walked through the Jordan, leaving the wilderness forever behind; but they are now confronted with a massive problem and face an enormous test. Satan is alive and active and wants to rob us of our new-found joy and victory. Suddenly, after the act of faith in crossing Jordan, we are in a major battle.

After Jesus was baptized he was led by the Spirit into the wilderness to be tempted by the devil. The blessing at the river was followed by a severe trial. After the blessing, the battle; after the fullness, the fight. Faith must be tested. In 1 Peter 5:7 we are told to cast all our care upon Jesus. There is the act of faith; yet immediately afterwards, in verse 8, we read: 'Be sober, be vigilant; because your adversary the devil walks about like a roaring lion, seeking whom he may devour.' Cast your all on God, trust him fully—and now remember, you have an enemy! 'Resist him, steadfast in the faith' (v. 9). 'Resist the devil and he will flee from you' (James 4:7). — Colin N. Peckham, *Joshua: A Devotional Commentary, Exploring the Bible Commentary* (Leominster, UK: Day One Publications, 2007), 110–111.

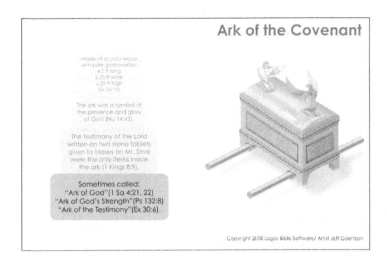

Ark of the Covenant

Made of acacia wood
with pure gold overlay:
4.5 ft long
2.25 ft wide
2.25 ft high
[Ex 25:10]

The ark was a symbol of
the presence and glory
of God [Nu 14:43].

The testimony of the Lord
written on two stone tablets
given to Moses on Mt. Sinai
were the only items inside
the ark (1 Kings 8:9).

Sometimes called:
"Ark of God"(1 Sa 4:21, 22)
"Ark of God's Strength"(Ps 132:8)
"Ark of the Testimony"(Ex 30:6).

Copyright 2008 Logos Bible Software/ Artist Jeff Goertzen

17. Verse 18. What are the devoted things?

The Hebrew word herem (devoted) means something
separated or banned from ordinary use. In Leviticus 27:21
it was a field and in Numbers 18:13 the firstfruits. The
actual practice of herem was important but not nearly as
important as its theological meaning. God wanted Israel to
be a separated people, set apart from the evil Canaanites.
He made clear that this was not possible if they began to
assimilate Canaanite culture into their own nation and
religion. Once again, this is a great lesson about worldliness in
our day.

No new warning here. Deuteronomy 20:16-18 says:

However, in the cities of the nations the Lord your God is
giving you as an inheritance, do not leave alive anything that
breathes. Completely destroy them—the Hittites, Amorites,
Canaanites, Perizzites, Hivites and Jebusites—as the Lord
your God has commanded you. Otherwise, they will teach
you to follow all the detestable things they do in worshiping
their gods, and you will sin against the Lord your God.

That's the warning; Joshua 6:18 offers the threat: Otherwise
you will make the camp of Israel liable to destruction and

bring trouble on it. — *Holman Old Testament Commentary – Joshua.*

18. What was the story of Rahab? Why was she spared?

Rahab hides the two Israelite spies from authorities who have heard reports that the spies were seen entering her house. Having set a false trail for the authorities, Rahab asks for protection from the spies, believing that the God of the Israelites will destroy her city. She helps the spies escape by letting them down outside the city wall and warning them which road to take to avoid capture. When Jericho falls, she and her family alone of all the people of Jericho are spared. Her family is blended into the nation and she becomes a distant relative of King David, and ultimately a part of the line of the Messiah, Jesus Christ (Matthew 1:5). — Jim George, *10 Minutes to Knowing the Men & Women of the Bible* (Eugene, OR: Harvest House, 2010).

19. What is the lesson here? Is this a story about how following God is passive—letting go and letting God work?

The tactics vary from situation to situation, but the principle remains the same. The previous generation had been taught the same lessons when they first came out of Egypt. Led by God himself to their camp place, facing the sea, with an impassable barrier in front of them and Pharaoh's elite troops closing in on them from behind, Moses instructs them, "Fear not, stand firm [or still], and see the salvation of the LORD, which he will work for you today.... The LORD will fight for you, and you have only to be silent [or still]" (Exodus 14:13, 14). The sea parts, the people cross, and as the pursuing Egyptians are doomed, Israel knows that she has been delivered by supernatural power alone. But when, three chapters later, they are attacked by the Amalekites at Rephidim, Moses instructs Joshua, "Choose for us men, and go out and fight with Amalek," and the outcome is that "Joshua overwhelmed Amalek and his people with the sword" (Exodus 17:8–13). Of course, the divine element is not absent even if the human activity is far more dominant.

The battle only flows Israel's way as Moses' hands are lifted up to Heaven, carrying the rod of God as a physical sign of their exclusive dependence on the power of the Lord to deliver his people from their enemies. The memory of this, written in a book and recited "in the ears of Joshua" (Exodus 17:14), would undoubtedly have had a profound influence on the military and spiritual education of this young warrior. And now, at Jericho, the lessons are indicative of exactly the same principle. — David Jackman, *Joshua: People of God's Purpose, ed. R. Kent Hughes, Preaching the Word* (Wheaton, IL: Crossway, 2014), 68.

20. What do you want to recall from today's conversation?

21. How can we support one another in prayer this week?

Joshua, Lesson #4
Good Questions Have Small Groups Talking
www.joshhunt.com

Joshua 7

OPEN

Let's each share your name and, did you ever steal anything as a child?

DIG

1. **Overview. Let's read this story as a whole, then let I will call on one of you to summarize it.**

   The sinner (Josh. 7:1). His name was Achan, or Achar, which means "trouble"; and he was from the tribe of Judah (v. 16). (See 1 Chron. 2:7; note in v. 26 that "Achor" also means "trouble.") He is known in Bible history as the man who troubled Israel (Josh. 7:25). Because of Achan's disobedience, Israel was defeated at Ai, and the enemy killed thirty-six Jewish soldiers. It was Israel's first and only military defeat in Canaan, a defeat that is forever associated with Achan's name.

   Never underestimate the amount of damage one person can do outside the will of God. Abraham's disobedience in Egypt almost cost him his wife (Gen. 12:10–20); David's disobedience in taking an unauthorized census led to the death of 70,000 people (2 Sam. 24); and Jonah's refusal to obey God almost sank a ship (Jonah 1). The church today must look diligently "lest any root of bitterness springing up cause trouble" (Heb. 12:15, NKJV). That's why Paul admonished the Corinthian believers to discipline the disobedient man in their fellowship, because his sin was defiling the whole church (1 Cor. 5). — Warren W. Wiersbe, *Be Strong, "Be" Commentary Series* (Wheaton, IL: Victor Books, 1996), 81–83.

2. How does this campaign differ from Jericho?

First, God gave Joshua an order to defeat Jericho and promised that He would give the city into Joshua's hand. Second, God gave Joshua the military strategy by which the victory could be won (see Josh. 6). The victory was God's, and He received full glory for it.

God no doubt had a battle plan for Ai, but Joshua didn't ask to hear it. Instead he sent out spies, and when they came back with a report that Ai could easily be taken, he dispatched a few thousand men without consulting God. He relied solely on human opinion.

In addition, God had commanded that the people not touch the "accursed things" of Jericho—items considered unclean according to the Law, including various personal effects. They were to take only the silver, gold, bronze, and iron vessels for the house of the Lord, and burn the rest (Josh. 6:18). A man named Achan did not obey. He brought accursed things into the camp, including a beautiful Babylonian garment. He also took two hundred shekels of silver and wedges of gold for himself, burying them in the ground beneath his tent.

Had Joshua listened for the Lord's counsel before moving against Ai, no doubt God would have revealed to him Achan's sin. The problem could have and should have been resolved before the assault on Ai. If it had been, no doubt the Israelites would have enjoyed another great success, again without any loss of Israelite life. — Charles F. Stanley, *The Charles F. Stanley Life Principles Bible: New King James Version* (Nashville, TN: Nelson Bibles, 2005), Jos 7:1–13.

3. What kind of town was Ai? To what town would you compare it?

Observe the report of the spies. "Aw, don't sweat this one, Joshua! Let's give most of the troops a break. They can use it after Jericho. We don't need more than two, maybe three thousand warriors. This is nothing." The report sounded like the Oklahoma Sooners were about to meet a squad of Cub Scouts on the football field. Either the report was accurate, or it reflected gross overconfidence.

Based on how the story unfolds, I believe the report was reasonable. Even the name Ai means "ruin." Just how impressive could this little town have been? Part of being a wise general is knowing how much of your resources to commit to a campaign. Joshua's not so foolish as to throw everything he's got into every battle. So to keep his troops fresh and to protect the camp, he sent only what seemed necessary—about three thousand men to sack Ai. Unfortunately, they were in for the mother of all shocks! — Charles R. Swindoll, *Fascinating Stories of Forgotten Lives* (Nashville: Thomas Nelson, 2005).

4. Who sinned, causing this judgment?

God made it clear that it was Israel that had sinned and not just Achan alone (Josh. 7:1, 11). Why would God blame the whole nation for the disobedience of only one soldier? Because Israel was one people in the Lord and not just an assorted collection of tribes, clans, families, and individuals. God dwelt in the midst of their camp, and this made the Jews the Lord's special people (Ex. 19:5–6). Jehovah God walked about in their camp, and therefore the camp was to be kept holy (Deut. 23:14). Anyone who disobeyed God defiled the camp, and this defilement affected their relationship to the Lord and to one another.

God's people today are one body in Christ. Consequently, we belong to each other, we need each other, and we affect each other (1 Cor. 12:12ff). Any weakness or infection in one part of the human body contributes to weakness and infection in the other parts. So it also is with the body of Christ. "If one part suffers, every part suffers with it; if one part is honored, every part rejoices with it" (1 Cor. 12:26, NIV). "One sinner destroys much good" (Ecc. 9:18, NKJV). — Warren W. Wiersbe, *Be Strong, "Be" Commentary Series* (Wheaton, IL: Victor Books, 1996), 83–84.

5. What was the sin?

The sin (Josh. 7:20–21). Achan heard his commander give the order that all the spoils in Jericho were to be devoted to the Lord and were to go into His treasury (6:17–21, 24). Since Jericho was Israel's first victory in Canaan, the firstfruits of the spoils belonged to the Lord (Prov. 3:9). But Achan disobeyed and took the hazardous steps that lead to sin and death (James 1:13–15): "I saw ... I coveted ... [I] took" (Josh. 7:21). Eve did the same thing when she listened to the devil (Gen. 3:5), and so did David when he yielded to the flesh (2 Sam. 11:1–4). Since Achan also coveted the things of the world, he brought defeat to Israel and death to himself and his family.
— Warren W. Wiersbe, *Be Strong, "Be" Commentary Series* (Wheaton, IL: Victor Books, 1996), 84.

6. Verse 1. What is a devoted thing?

However, the whole idea of the "devoted things" was designed to teach Israel lessons of holiness and separation, which had been on God's agenda ever since he met Moses in the burning bush at Sinai and commanded him to take off his sandals since he was standing on holy ground. We tend to think of holiness in somewhat limited ethical terms as the word that describes God's perfect moral righteousness. Certainly it does that, but in doing so it becomes a key word that distinguishes God from his creation. Holiness speaks of his sheer "otherness," not only in moral perfection, but in all the divine attributes that separate the Creator from the creature. It is the word that describes the very Godness of God. So to be allied with this supreme divine being demands of his people a set-apartness or separation that reflects their otherness as distinct from an unbelieving and rebellious world. Where that rebellion is relentlessly pursued, as in Canaanite paganism, it must eventually be set apart for destruction. But where the redeemed community of sinners, who have been redeemed by the blood of God's appointed sacrifice, are concerned, they are to be set apart as the Lord's own special possession, to live as reflections of his perfect holiness among "a crooked and twisted generation" (Philippians 2:15). That is our calling too, as Paul is making clear, as the new covenant community. — David Jackman, *Joshua: People of God's Purpose, ed. R. Kent Hughes, Preaching the Word* (Wheaton, IL: Crossway, 2014), 78.

7. Verses 2 – 5. What happened as a result of Achan's sin?

This is the unhappy heading for verses 2–5, where sadly everything seems to be going wrong. What we must realize is that the sequence of events is the outcome of the Lord's anger burning against them. This is what Israel will be like if God is no longer with them—very human and very vulnerable. Throughout the narrative there are valid parallels with what happens to the new covenant community, the church, when God's truth is compromised by human rebellion against his divine word. If our message is progressively disregarded or trashed by the prevailing cultural ethos, so that the church becomes known for its ineffectiveness and its capitulation to the enemies of truth, should we not ask ourselves whether this represents a withdrawal of God's presence in blessing because of our compromise and sometimes outright rejection of his word? — David Jackman, *Joshua: People of God's Purpose, ed. R. Kent Hughes, Preaching the Word* (Wheaton, IL: Crossway, 2014), 79.

8. Locate Ai on a map.

9. Verse 5. How is Israel feeling after this defeat?

The comment of verse 5 that "the hearts of the people melted and became as water" is a poignant, ironic echo of Rahab's comment in 2:11 ("our hearts melted, and there was no spirit left in any man because of you") or the narrator's comment in 5:1 that when the kings of the Amorites and the Canaanites "heard that the LORD had dried up the waters of the Jordan for the people of Israel until they had crossed over, their hearts melted and there was no longer any spirit in them because of the people of Israel." Now the boot is on the other foot. Now it is Israel's turn to feel the helplessness and then the panic bred by defeat. There is not a Christian who has not been there, when our disobedience or unfaithfulness to God's word has brought about a total lack

of confidence and coherence in our spiritual lives, and our hearts melted with fear. But that is where we will always be as sinful people living in a fallen world if God's gospel smile is turned away because of our unconfessed sin. Then even our prayer mocks us because, as the psalmist testifies, "If I had cherished iniquity in my heart, the Lord would not have listened" (Psalm 66:18). The only way through such despair is the guilty person's cry for grace, "God, be merciful to me, a sinner!" (Luke 18:13). The only way to be justified is to turn

from our sin and failure and cast ourselves upon God's mercy.
— David Jackman, *Joshua: People of God's Purpose*, ed. R.
Kent Hughes, Preaching the Word (Wheaton, IL: Crossway,
2014), 80.

10. Verse 6. What is the significance of tearing his clothes?

After tearing his clothes (a sign of distress and mourning; see
Gen. 37:29, 34), Joshua speaks to the Lord for the first time
in the chapter, raising his urgent complaint and accusing
the Lord of bringing this people over the Jordan ... to give us
into the hands of the Amorites (Josh. 7:7). Joshua's words
carry the further implication that the Lord has reversed
his repeated promise (ch. 1) to give both the land and the
inhabitants of Canaan into Israel's hands. Joshua's fear that
our name will be cut off ... from the earth (7:9) hints at a
further reversal, namely, of the Lord's promise to Abraham
to "make your name great" (Gen. 12:2). If these promises
fail, Joshua insists, they will do little for your great name (on
the issue of Israel's fate and the Lord's reputation, see Num.
14:13–16; Deut. 9:26–29). But Joshua is about to learn that
his probing questions are misdirected. — Crossway Bibles,
The ESV Study Bible (Wheaton, IL: Crossway Bibles, 2008),
404.

11. Verses 6 – 9. What was Joshua's concern in this prayer?

What a great leader! His first reaction was grief for the fallen
men, then for the nation's future, and ultimately for the
integrity of God's name, His reputation. I love that kind of
reasoning. His actions and passionate prayer implied: "Lord,
I'm not worried about my reputation as a leader. This is Your
battle. Your name is at stake."

The man at the top, none other than the commander in chief,
poured out his heart before the Lord because he had come
upon a mystery. The defeat at Ai was humanly inexplicable,
militarily baffling, and from all that Joshua knew, completely
illogical from a spiritual perspective. That's why his first
question to God was, "Why did You ever bring this people

over the Jordan, only to deliver us into the hand of the Amorites, to destroy us?" So this spiritual leader took the only logical course of action when defeat occurs. He took it to the Lord.

There's a lesson for leaders here. This applies to any leader who follows God, whether in business or ministry. In the face of mysterious defeat, put the brakes on, stop everything, and take the time to look up. Ask the Lord God to reveal the reason.

I've gone through periods in my own ministry when back-to-back defeats that made no sense baffled me. This would happen after the team had planned carefully, prayed through the preparation, and moved forward with deliberate, calculated, faithful confidence in the Lord's direction . . . only to suffer an Ai kind of defeat. Occasionally, after prayer and a period of soul-searching analysis, the Lord (some might call it happenstance) uncovered sin in the camp. I cannot adequately describe the chilling disbelief and the utter heartache you suffer upon discovering that a trusted colleague has betrayed the ministry, your friendship, and even the Lord. I'm confident that some of you reading this know the horror of betrayal all too well. It leaves you reeling.

Since this dreadful experience still occurs, we'd be wise to take our time and watch the following events transpire. What occurred on Joshua's watch is worth careful analysis. — Charles R. Swindoll, *Fascinating Stories of Forgotten Lives* (Nashville: Thomas Nelson, 2005).

12. Circle the word "devoted" if you have the NIV, or "under the ban" as the NASB has it. What does that mean?

The cherem, translated "the ban," was not a complicated concept. Rather than hoard the spoils of victory for themselves, the soldiers were to take nothing home. Everything living was to have been put to death. Everything valuable was to have been put in the treasury of the Lord. Everything was set apart for Him. Simple.

Ushers receiving an offering in a church have a similar code. The ushers don't say, "Well, if I were being paid to do this very important job for the church, I think thus-and-such amount would be fair compensation. I'll take out a little less than that so, in the end, the church is coming out ahead. After all, if no one did this job, the church would receive no money at all."

That looks stupid just reading it, doesn't it? No one in his right mind would expect that logic to work. In fact, the integrity of most people carrying out this function in church is so high that none of them even wants to be alone with the money. That way the whole process remains above reproach and every penny is tallied, accounted for, and given to the Lord.

Unfortunately for Israel, someone after the battle of Jericho had emptied a full offering plate into his own pockets. Joshua was innocent. The vast majority of Israel was blameless. Still, the entire nation suffered. J. Sidlow Baxter describes the effect this way: "The electric wire of fellowship between God and Israel had been cut and the current of power therefore ceased to flow." That's precisely the consequence of sin in the camp. That's also why I think the intelligence report on the strength of Ai was a reasonable one. This should have been an easy victory, even without the Lord's involvement. No miracle needed there, but the presence of sin interrupted God's desire to bless the nation with another victory. — Charles R. Swindoll, *Fascinating Stories of Forgotten Lives* (Nashville: Thomas Nelson, 2005).

13. Verse 21. What do we learn about sin from this verse?

Achan's first mistake was to look at these spoils a second time. He probably couldn't help seeing them the first time, but he should never have looked again and considered taking them. A man's first glance at a woman may say to him, "She's attractive!" But it's that second glance that gets the imagination working and leads to sin (Matt. 6:27–30). If we keep God's Word before our eyes, we won't start looking in the wrong direction and doing the wrong things (Prov. 4:20–

25). — Warren W. Wiersbe, *Be Strong, "Be" Commentary Series* (Wheaton, IL: Victor Books, 1996), 84.

14. How do you imagine Achan justified this thievery?

Do not miss the downward spiral of Achan's sin.

"I saw . . .

I coveted . . .

I took . . .

I hid."

That's the way it happens. But he failed to see the final phase of the progression: "I got caught." We rarely think of that one before we sin. Only after, when the paranoia sets in.

At the time of his sin, Achan probably thought something along these lines of rationalization. "My family and I have been deprived of many good things during our years of wilderness living. Here is this beautiful, new, stylish garment, a little bit of silver, and a handful of gold. This is no big deal. God will never miss this in light of all the treasury that we'll haul back from Jericho. I fought hard, so I'm entitled to a few enjoyable things in life, after all."

I realize that I'm speculating, but that's how the human mind works. Carnality can be incredibly inventive when it comes to rationalizing sin. In the heat of the moment, the excitement of hidden sin, the adventure, the forbidden pleasure drives away all reason. We see, we covet, we take, and we hide.
— Charles R. Swindoll, *Fascinating Stories of Forgotten Lives* (Nashville: Thomas Nelson, 2005).

15. What is the lesson for us in verse 21?

Achan's confession in Josh. 7:21 contains an instructive progression of verbs: He saw, coveted, took, then hid. His sin was not in seeing the robe, silver, and gold, but he permitted his eyes not only to glance, but also to gaze upon these forbidden treasures.

Achan would not have hidden what he had not taken. He would not have taken what he had not coveted. He would not have coveted what he had not seen. And while he could not, perhaps, avoid the initial glance, he could certainly have avoided the prolonged gaze that fed his lust for what was not his. — *Discipleship Journal.*

16. Coveting is the last of the Ten Commandments. What bad things happen when we covet?

God also knows that covetousness feeds itself and leads to greater sin. Remember Achan, who misappropriated a beautiful robe, about five pounds of silver, and one and a quarter pounds of gold? First he saw them, then he coveted them, and then he took them (Josh. 7:21). His sin led to the deaths of about 36 Israelites in the battle of Ai (Josh. 7:5).

Knowing how powerful covetousness is, Jesus said, "Watch out! Be on your guard against all forms of greed; a man's life does not consist in the abundance of his possessions" (Lk. 12:15). He also said, "For from within, out of men's hearts, come evil thoughts... greed" (Mk. 7:21-22).

What forms of covetousness do our lives display? Have I ever wished that I was driving another man's car? Yes. Have I ever looked at another man's house and longed to own it instead of our "fix-up" home? Yes. Have I ever seen a person flashing a wad of bills around and wished that I had that money? Yes. After talking with many other believers, I know I'm not alone. And our materialistic society fuels our sinful desires.

When we covet others' possessions several things happen. We become discontent with what God has provided for us instead of being thankful. We take our eyes off God and His provision and concentrate on obtaining what we desire. And often our desires become hotter, which can cause us to sin in other ways as Satan pries open our hidden thoughts and urges us to act on them—to disobey God. — *Discipleship Journal.*

17. Verses 16 – 18. Why didn't God just tell Joshua who did it?

It occurs to me that God simply could have given the name of the thief to Joshua instead of orchestrating this very elaborate, very public search. Perhaps in His grace, He was giving the man every opportunity to step up, confess, repent, spare the community any further suffering, and take his punishment. Still, through it all, the guilty man said nothing. His sin remained buried.

Before we go on, allow me to point out, once again, the public nature of the thief's sin. Some sins become a very public scandal, the kind that ruins ministries forever. Even when the personalities are gone, a dark cloud shrouds the reputation of the organization in suspicion and cynicism. But let's admit that most sins are private in the sense that no one knows about them but you and God—no one but me and God. In this case, God wanted it handled publicly.

The manhunt continued in progressively smaller concentric circles as the Lord had Joshua cast lots to fine-tune his search. In the Old Testament, before the Holy Spirit took up permanent residence in the hearts of believers, this was the process for determining God's will. Not unlike rolling dice, the priest played a game of chance, as it were, except that God controlled the outcome, and the stakes made it anything but a gamble. With each round, the noose tightened around the thief's neck. First by tribe, then by family, then by household, then man by man.

Finally, the elimination search left only one man, naked in his sin before the whole camp. The thief was discovered. The finger of undisputed accusation finally pointed at Achan. — Charles R. Swindoll, *Fascinating Stories of Forgotten Lives* (Nashville: Thomas Nelson, 2005).

18. Verse 19. How do you think this felt for Joshua?

My heart is heavy for Joshua as I read again this account of a leader having to confront sin in the camp. As I read, I find myself reliving those few, awful occasions in ministry when I had to sit face to face with someone who had buried a secret sin and told a lie that damaged a ministry and destroyed a family. Each confrontation was different. Sometimes it takes a person hours to come out with the truth. With others, the confession gushes out immediately with a rush of tears, as in Achan's case. — Charles R. Swindoll, *Fascinating Stories of Forgotten Lives* (Nashville: Thomas Nelson, 2005).

19. What happened to Achan?

Joshua used an interesting play on words with Achan's name, which in Hebrew, interestingly, means "trouble." "Why have you lived up to your name, Achan?" Then they took him to a place called Achor, which comes from the same root, meaning "place of trouble," and Israel executed justice. After executing Achan and all the people who helped him conceal his sin, their possessions were burned in accordance with God's command, and their graves marked by memorial stones so that no one would forget.

Shocking, isn't it? Such harshness offends our modern sensibilities, softened by compromise. Our reaction is either to minimize the severity by glossing over the details or to recoil in fear from a God who could be so severe. How different it would be in our politically correct day. Attorneys would defend Achan by declaring him temporarily insane or by finding a technical loophole. ("Joshua failed to read the man his rights!") Or they might have him plead guilty to petty theft and plea bargain a lighter sentence rather than involve the whole camp in a lengthy, expensive trial. Public opinion might come to the rescue. "He apologized and returned the goods. What purpose does an execution serve? It would be inhumane. Furthermore, will it restore the thirty-six fallen soldiers to their families?"

We live in the age of grace, but some would twist that concept into a license to sin. Many others would redefine sin to exclude any act that doesn't hurt someone else. In their words, sin isn't something that defies God; sin is something that harms others. Yet, I can find nowhere in Scripture anything to suggest that an action has to hurt someone else in order for God to consider it a sin.

For that matter, I cannot find any indication, either in Scripture or in my experience, that sin is ever isolated. Not really. Private perhaps, but never isolated. Sin, to some degree, always affects others. Just because we can't build a logical, cause-and-effect case every time, doesn't make that any less true. As a pastor, I have seen one person's "private" sin break the hearts of family members as well as hinder the work of an entire church. As a nation we have seen more than one president's "private" sin corrupt an administration. Sin in the camp is a powerful enemy to a fruitful ministry. Satan would love nothing more than to keep that sin buried, convince us that our choices are nobody's business but our own, and let it rot our lives from the inside out. The Adversary's logic feeds on such deception.

One individual who continues to walk in darkness—contrary to the mind of God—can erode the effectiveness of an entire organization and steal any hope of victory. One Judas can affect an entire group of disciples. One Achan can stop a nation in its tracks. One person with unconfessed, unrepentant, unresolved sin buried in his or her tent can have untold negative impact on everything and everyone he or she touches. Sin in the camp is deadly, even in this age of grace.
— Charles R. Swindoll, *Fascinating Stories of Forgotten Lives* (Nashville: Thomas Nelson, 2005).

20. Application. What is the lesson for us in this story?

As I observe the story of the man whose sin brought calamity, and compare it to my own experience in ministry leadership, I want to leave you with three serious principles to consider. Because we live in a fallen, broken, twisted world, you are likely in one of three situations. You may be the leader of an organization with sin in the camp. (Don't become suspicious, but please do remain alert.) You may be a member of an organization with sin in the camp. Or you may be the one nurturing sin. You have it buried in your tent, and when no one is looking, you dig it up to caress it. Whatever your position, consider these three principles.

First, sin in the camp stinks, and others can detect its unique stench. I've chosen those words carefully. I realize they are somewhat crude, but they're appropriate. There is a unique stench, there's a smell about suspicion. Interestingly, the closer we walk with God, the more quickly we catch the nauseating odor. A tender heart that is intimate with God is particularly sensitive to the presence of sin. This can easily become twisted into fear and habitual suspicion. Let's not go there. No one is immune to Satan's deception, and we can't go about jumping at every shadow. But trust your gut instincts. Intuition is rarely wrong.

Don't be thickheaded as a spiritual leader. If inexplicable defeat and decline begins to plague your ministry with no logical explanation, pay attention. Wake up and smell the roses . . . or better, the rubbish. It may or may not be the result of sin in the camp, but don't be naive. Do what Joshua did. Take it before the Lord with complete candor and humility. Lean hard upon Him. Ask Him to open a window from His heavenly perspective. Remember that this is His battle, and that He will protect what belongs to Him, including His reputation.

If you, my friend, are the Achan of your family or ministry or company or (you fill in the blank) . . . if you are nurturing a secret sin, don't think others can't smell the stench. They may not be able to place the source—not yet, anyway—but the pungent odor of your sin hangs in the air. And it quite likely keeps the people around you from experiencing victory.

Repent. Today! Don't delay. Decide now that this sin must go. Remember our opening section of Scripture? — Charles R. Swindoll, *Fascinating Stories of Forgotten Lives* (Nashville: Thomas Nelson, 2005).

21. How can we support one another in prayer this week?

Prayer is not a convenient device for imposing our will upon God, or bending his will to ours, but the prescribed way of subordinating our will to his. —John Stott

Prayer is the spiritual gymnasium in which we exercise and practice godliness. —V. L. Crawford

The great tragedy of life is not unanswered prayer, but unoffered prayer. —F. B. Meyer

Campus Life's Ignite Your Faith, *Ignite Your Faith: 365 Devotions to Set Your Faith on Fire* (Grand Rapids, MI: Revell, 2009).

Joshua, Lesson #5
Good Questions Have Small Groups Talking
www.joshhunt.com

If you could email your group and ask them to read this chapter, along with any notes they might have from a study Bible, it will make for a more informed discussion.

Joshua 22.10 - 34

OPEN

Let's each share your name and, what is one object you have at your house that helps you to remember the Lord. Perhaps you have a cross or other piece of Christian art.

DIG

1. **Joshua 22.10 – 12. They people of Israel nearly had a civil war. Why?**

   As we will see in verses 27 and 28, the Israelites on the east side of the Jordan built an altar not for sacrifice or worship, but, rather, as a symbol of their solidarity with their brothers on the west side of the Jordan. So incensed by this were their brothers on the west side, however, that civil war nearly ensued.

   The nine and one-half tribes were in the Promised Land, but the enemy sought to divide them from their brothers on the other side of the Jordan. Satan's strategy is still the same: divide and conquer. His goal is always to get believers to separate, to distance, to analyze. In this passage, we see four ways the nine and one-half tribes fell prey to the destructive division that almost led to civil war... — Jon Courson, *Jon Courson's Application Commentary: Volume One: Genesis–Job* (Nashville, TN: Thomas Nelson, 2005), 699.

2. What do we learn about conflict—and how to avoid it—from this story?

The first step towards division was taken when the nine and one-half tribes acted on hearsay. They didn't see the altar the two and one-half tribes had built—they only heard about it. That's always how Satan begins to bring people into division and opposition. So often, divisions in families or churches are based simply on what is heard. Rumors take on a life of their own and fires are fanned when people act on hearsay. — Jon Courson, *Jon Courson's Application Commentary: Volume One: Genesis–Job* (Nashville, TN: Thomas Nelson, 2005), 699.

3. Someone look up Proverbs 18.13. How could they have benefited from listening to this Proverb?

The second mistake of the nine and one-half tribes was that they got worked up before they checked the situation out. That is, they sharpened their swords and grabbed their shields before they established the facts. "He that answers a matter before he hears it, it is a folly and a shame unto him" (Proverbs 18:13). Making a decision without learning the whole story leads to folly and shame ultimately. — Jon Courson, *Jon Courson's Application Commentary: Volume One: Genesis–Job* (Nashville, TN: Thomas Nelson, 2005), 699.

4. Can you think of other Proverbs that help us deal with conflict?

A hot-tempered man stirs up conflict, but a man slow to anger calms strife. Proverbs 15:18 (HCSB)

A contrary man spreads conflict, and a gossip separates close friends. Proverbs 16:28 (HCSB)

To start a conflict is to release a flood; stop the dispute before it breaks out. Proverbs 17:14 (HCSB)

Drive out a mocker, and conflict goes too; then quarreling and dishonor will cease. Proverbs 22:10 (HCSB)

Without wood, fire goes out; without a gossip, conflict dies down. Proverbs 26:20 (HCSB)

A greedy person provokes conflict, but whoever trusts in the LORD will prosper. Proverbs 28:25 (HCSB)

An angry man stirs up conflict, and a hot-tempered man increases rebellion. Proverbs 29:22 (HCSB)

5. Why did the Reubenites, the Gadites and the half-tribe of Manasseh build this altar? What was their motive?

We do not know exactly where Geliloth stood, but we can make a safe assumption that it was near Gilgal where they had first entered the land. That would have been southeast of Shiloh and familiar territory. With the purest of motives, the warriors of the two and one-half tribes built an imposing altar there by the Jordan. We learn later that they wanted some visible reminder of the union of the tribes and of their right and obligation to come back to Shiloh for worship. Presumably the altar could be seen across the river from the eastern bank as well as by the tribes living in Canaan.

So far in the text this behavior doesn't alarm us, but it certainly did the western tribes. They were concerned about the site that was in territory belonging to Manasseh or Benjamin, but they were much more concerned about the significance. What could have been so bad about this altar to cause them to think immediately about going to war against them? — *Holman Old Testament Commentary – Joshua.*

6. Why did the other tribes think they had built this altar?

The problem was that the western tribes thought the eastern tribes had built their own place of worship that would be more convenient than going all the way to Shiloh. That was unacceptable to them because it violated the direct

61

command of God (Deut. 12:13-14). Although their reaction seems quick and harsh, at least the Israelites understood the danger of unfaithfulness. If this was an altar, the nation was in jeopardy.

Here we learn lessons both positive and negative. On the positive side, concern for faithfulness and strict adherence to God's law is commendable. Nevertheless, their knee-jerk response of considering war as the solution after they had fought shoulder to shoulder with these people for the last seven years seems outrageous. — *Holman Old Testament Commentary – Joshua.*

7. What did they do with their suspicion? Was that a good thing?

At least they decided to send a delegation to get to the bottom of the problem. The phrase whole assembly of Israel seems striking since Joshua has repeatedly acknowledged that the two and one-half tribes living east of the Jordan River were part of Israel as well. "A survey of the rest of the chapter reveals that the narrator and the speakers consistently maintain such a distinction until the misunderstanding about the altar has been explained in a satisfactory manner" (Howard, 407). Furthermore, the delegation headed by Phinehas did not meet the two and one-half tribes at the altar but in the land of Gilead. — *Holman Old Testament Commentary – Joshua.*

8. Joshua 22.15 – 20. How do you sense the tone of this conversation?

Suddenly "the whole assembly of Israel" (22:12) became the whole assembly of the Lord. Verbal excommunication had already taken place for these two and one-half tribes and the judgment had already been rendered: How could you break faith with the God of Israel like this? Phinehas remembered the sin of Peor back in Numbers 25 in which he played a significant role. In an emotional response, he has no intention of watching that kind of plague fall upon the nation again.

This business of crossing the Jordan River to worship was no small matter, for the Jordan is a river of some significance. Campbell tells us that

> ... mountains on each side rise to heights above 2,000 feet and the Jordan Valley nestled in between is in effect a great trench 5 to 15 miles wide. During a part of the year the intense heat greatly discourages travelers. This then was a very pronounced river boundary and may have contributed to the fear of these tribesmen that they and their brethren would permanently drift apart. After all, "out of sight" is often "out of mind" (Campbell, BKC, 365).

So the Phinehas delegation used strong language to describe what they believed to be a major spiritual failure, comparing it not only with Peor but with the sin of Achan, who acted unfaithfully regarding the devoted things.

Howard sees in the delegates' critical remarks

> ... the implication that Israel had never truly rid itself of this sin, that it always flirted with—if not participated in—idolatry and the allure of pagan religious systems. Achan's case was proof positive of this and the Cisjordan tribes feared that this altar represented another such case (Howard, 409).

But to their credit, the delegation offered a solution. If this altar had been built because the Transjordanian tribes were not happy with their land, then let them come over to the Lord's land, where the Lord's tabernacle stands, and share the land with us. Better to abandon physical material possessions including land and be close to worship than to allow distance from worship to corrupt one's life. This speech may indicate that the Canaan settlers never considered the land on the eastern side of the Jordan River to be a good choice. But Moses had given it to the two and one-half tribes, and Joshua had confirmed that allocation more than once. — *Holman Old Testament Commentary – Joshua.*

9. Proverbs 15.1. How important is tone to the successful resolution of conflict?

The Bible is full of life-transforming truths that affect our ability to get along. The first verse I ever memorized would go a long way toward helping us to get along with each other: "Be ye kind one to another." (Ephesians 4:32 KJV) We need to think clearly about the tone of our voices. Science in the Bible agree that the tone of your voice has as much to do with your ability to get along with others as just about anything. The Bible says, "let your gentleness be evident to all." (Philippians 4:5)

> For example, take a study where people were given performance feedback – some negative, some positive. If they were given negative performance feedback in a very warm, positive, and upbeat tone, they came out of there feeling pretty good about the interaction. If they were given positive feedback in a very cold, critical, judgmental tone, they came out feeling negative, even about positive feedback. So the emotional subtext is more powerful in many ways than the overt, ostensible interaction that we're having.

When your mind is transformed through the power of the Holy Spirit using the Word of God to change your mind so that your gentleness is evident to all, your relationships will start to change. You will find it is a whole lot easier to get along with others when your gentleness is evident to all. When you meditate on that truth, your life is changed, and your relationships change. People who were once hard to get along with become much easier to get along with as you meditate on the command to let your gentleness be evident to all.

We are transformed through the Bible's teaching on forgiveness. We are transformed by the Bible's teaching on gentleness. We are transformed by the Bible's teaching on squeaky-clean honesty. There is much, much more. We will explore what the Bible says about taming the tongue and about self-care. We will look at what the Bible teaches about empathy and listening. We will meditate together on what the Bible teaches about serving and about confronting when you need to confront. As we will see, getting along is not just being nice all the time. Sometimes, we need to turn over some tables. — Josh Hunt, *How to Get Along With Almost Anyone*, 2014.

10. Back to Joshua 22.15 – 20. What did they do right here?

Consider the three characteristics of this appeal by the Phinehas delegation:

It was personal. Instead of marching on the tribes, the Israelites chose a delegation headed by a priest. They delivered a sincere message before they picked a fight. That's a good approach.

It was passionate. The Israelites made the trip because they were concerned about faithfulness to God. They guarded God's reputation and holiness and his command about the central altar. By appealing to Peor and Achan, they recalled the time when Moabite worship brought a plague on the whole nation and twenty-four thousand Israelites died. They also remembered the time when the first battle for Ai was hopelessly lost. This delegation pled, begged, and tried to turn the eastern tribes from what they considered to be sin. Their motive was pure, even if their reasoning was faulty.

It was purposeful. The option of land grants west of the Jordan River shows a desire to restore these tribes and bring them back to a place where they could keep their commitment to God. Though wrong-headed, this whole process was right hearted. — *Holman Old Testament Commentary – Joshua.*

11. Verses 21ff. What was the tone of this response?

The reply of the tribes east of the Jordan is heartwarming and enormously encouraging (vv. 21–29). They begin with an ascription of glory to God, repeated for solemnity and emphasis—"The Mighty One, God, the Lord!" (v. 22a). At the very start of their reply the eastern tribes affirm that their confession of Yahweh as God of gods is exactly the same as their western brothers. He is the one before whom they stand, and their loyalty to him is total. "He knows; and let Israel itself know!" (v. 22). In other words, "What we want you to hear and understand about our position or actions is something that is clearly known by God and open to his all-seeing eye." He knows the integrity of their hearts, and they are able to call on him as a witness to the truth of the explanation they are about to give. If their intention had been to set up a rival shrine to the tabernacle or an alternative to the sacrificial system, they freely admit, they deserve to die (vv. 22b, 23a), and they would fully expect the Lord to take vengeance (v. 23b). That was neither their motivation nor intention. — David Jackman, *Joshua: People of God's Purpose*, ed. R. Kent Hughes, *Preaching the Word* (Wheaton, IL: Crossway, 2014), 170.

12. What was the real reason for this altar?

The following verses explain the real reason for the altar's construction. Because the River Jordan formed such a significant physical barrier between them and the rest of the nation, they were afraid it might create a division between them in future generations. Their service on behalf of the western tribes could easily be forgotten when their generation had passed on; so they thought that some visible reminder was needed. If later generations west of the river began to imagine that the easterners had no right to worship the Lord at the tabernacle ("no portion in the Lord," vv. 25, 27) because they did not live in the land, then their children would be excluded from fellowship with Yahweh, with all the obvious disastrous results that implied (v. 25). The altar then was built not as a place of sacrifice but as a witness. At last the skilful storyteller brings us to the narrative's climax, which resolves the problem. The building of an altar as a memorial was not in any way meant to diminish the tabernacle but to show that these tribes were equally a part of Israel, equally dependent on the sacrificial system, and equally committed to the worship of Yahweh. This would be the ultimate answer to the questioning of their Israelite legitimacy by any future generations. The copy of the altar of the Lord is proof of their total integration within Israel, with their full covenant rights and privileges (v. 28). Their purpose was therefore the very opposite of what the eastern delegation had feared. Rather than rebellion, it was intended as a mark of loyalty and unity. — David Jackman, *Joshua: People of God's Purpose, ed. R. Kent Hughes, Preaching the Word* (Wheaton, IL: Crossway, 2014), 170–171.

13. What is the emotion in verse 30?

After their detailed explanation, the relief is almost palpable (v. 30). For the delegation "it was good in their eyes," exactly what they wanted to hear. Phinehas expresses their joy not only because the issue has been resolved but also because this happy and peaceful outcome is certain evidence that "the LORD is in our midst" (v. 31). The catastrophe has been averted; the loyalty of the eastern tribes is established beyond doubt; the wrath of God no longer hangs over the people. The delegation reports back to the western tribes, and it is "good in [their] eyes" too (v. 33). The threat of war is dropped, and the altar is allowed to stand. Indeed, it is given a more formal and enhanced status by the name that Reuben and Gad confer upon it—"Witness" (v. 34), or more fully, "it is a witness between us that the LORD is God." In this way it became a symbolic reaffirmation of the national unity of the twelve tribes, which is created and sustained by the fact that for them all Yahweh is Lord. — David Jackman, *Joshua: People of God's Purpose, ed. R. Kent Hughes, Preaching the Word* (Wheaton, IL: Crossway, 2014), 171.

14. Israel was able to maintain unity when things could have burst into conflict. What is the lesson for us in maintaining unity?

That is also the only source of unity for the contemporary Christian church, under the Lordship of Jesus Christ. True unity exists not through church councils or synods, not through resolutions or political bargaining, but in the simplest and most basic creed that is the heart of the gospel, namely that "Jesus is Lord" (1 Corinthians 12:3). That is the incontrovertible proof of the Holy Spirit's work. No other confession can unite sinners than that which is expressed by bowing to Christ's Lordship in every area of our life and experience. It is not even in Christ as Savior that the deepest unity is found, but when the Savior is exalted and worshipped as Lord. Indeed, it is only because he is the Lord that he can prove himself to be the Savior. When the rivalry to God's rule, which is endemic in our human nature, is finally laid at the feet of the crucified Lord, a unity between God and his people is created that is deeper and more lasting than the strongest earthly ties.

Of course, the ultimate fulfillment of that hope will be in the eternal kingdom. Our Christian unity will never be perfect on this earth since we still battle against the world, the flesh, and the devil. But the church needs a sharpened vision of what is possible, even in this world, as we submit to Christ and turn our backs on all rivals. In Bruce Waltke's acute and searching words, "If the absence of apostasy is a cause to praise God for his presence with his people (22:31), then its presence ought to prompt believers to investigate possible cause(s) of his disfavour." The presence of apostasy in so many forms within the visible church in the West must precipitate an increasing absence of God's presence and power in its life and witness. Where God is sidelined and his Word disregarded, his Spirit is grieved and may well withdraw until his people come to their senses in renewed repentance, loyalty, faith, and obedience. The Israelites were determined to deal with the issue because the continued presence of God in their midst was both their greatest blessing and their greatest need. Is our responsibility any less? — David Jackman, *Joshua: People of God's Purpose, ed. R. Kent Hughes, Preaching the Word* (Wheaton, IL: Crossway, 2014), 171–172.

15. What are some biblical keys to dealing with conflict?

A couple of years ago, I was harshly criticized by a nationally recognized Christian leader for something that had happened in my personal life. His comments, which were printed nationally, were very hurtful to me personally. I came to know in a very real way what Jesus meant when He used the phrase, "If ye have ought against any" (Mark 11:25 KJV).

Although this isn't the exact definition of that term in King James English, my definition is true to the meaning: When we have ought against a brother, we find ourselves saying such things as …

- "He ought to have behaved differently toward me."

- "He ought not to have said that about me."

- "He ought to have drawn different conclusions about my situation."

- "He ought to have kept his opinions about me and my future to himself."

What did I do with these feelings of "ought"—these feelings against my brother in Christ?

First, I called this man. I felt strongly that I needed to let him know that he had hurt me by his comments. He did not receive my first two calls but finally, I got him on the phone. I quickly realized that he had spoken without knowing any of the real facts of the situation. He had made a judgment without due process. He had self-appointed himself to be my prosecutor, judge, and jury.

I asked him why he hadn't let me know that he had felt offended by what had happened in my life. I asked him why he hadn't called me prior to making such hurtful comments about me in the public media. He had no answer.

Furthermore, he expressed no regret whatsoever for the pain he had caused me personally or professionally. I hung up the phone disappointed and, frankly, a little stunned. But I also hung up the phone knowing that I had done what was biblically correct. I had gone to this man with my personal grievance.

The next step I took was to forgive this man and let the matter drop. I didn't speak out against him or seek to retaliate, justify myself, or point out his errors. I refuse even now to tell who he was or what he said, or to discuss the situation that prompted his criticism. I let go of the anger, frustration, and hurt that I felt, and I said to the Lord, "He is Your concern. I trust You to deal with him in whatever way You choose."

How do you feel when you are criticized? Do you feel sad, angry, hurt, insecure, exposed, betrayed? How do you respond? Do you blame, accuse, stuff your emotions, or apologize?

Conflict is part of every person's life. It is found at home, work, school, in the neighborhood, between friends, at sports arenas, and yes, even in the church. We can't escape conflict. Rather, we need to learn how to deal with it and respond to it. In nearly all cases, conflict, misunderstanding, and criticism go together, at least to a degree. — Charles F. Stanley, *Walking Wisely: Real Guidance for Life's Journey* (Nashville, TN: Thomas Nelson Publishers, 2002), 204–207.

16. Is it possible for us to live a conflict-free life?

Conflict can never be avoided completely. If conflict could have been avoided, Jesus certainly would have chosen a different route. So would Paul and all of the first apostles of Jesus. God never promises any person a life free of conflict. He never commands us to avoid conflict. Rather, God admonishes us to learn how to respond to conflict in a godly manner. — Charles F. Stanley, *Walking Wisely: Real Guidance for Life's Journey* (Nashville, TN: Thomas Nelson Publishers, 2002), 207.

17. Would you say conflict is inevitable?

Even though conflict can never be fully avoided, it is not inevitable among rivals or equals. Some people assume that just because two people are equal in their talents or achievements, they must be rivals or be in open conflict with each other. That isn't at all the case. In fact, as Christians we are to live in harmony with our fellow believers. We are not to set ourselves up to be in competitive conflict.

In the early days of our nation, two giants of the faith, John Wesley and George Whitefield, led major revival movements that resulted in thousands of people accepting Christ as their Savior. One day a man asked John Wesley if he thought he would see George Whitefield in heaven. Wesley replied, "No, I do not." The man asked again, "Are you telling me that you don't believe George Whitefield is a converted man?"

Wesley replied, "I do not believe that I will see him in heaven, because he will be so close to the throne, and I will be so far away that I will never see him."

Although they disagreed doctrinally, these two men refused to criticize each other or to engage in personal conflict. Neither man gave evidence of being motivated by envy of the other. — Charles F. Stanley, *Walking Wisely: Real Guidance for Life's Journey* (Nashville, TN: Thomas Nelson Publishers, 2002), 208.

18. Is conflict evidence of sin?

At times, conflict arises through simple neglect or an innocent mistake. Not all conflict is rooted in willful behavior. Furthermore, conflict can result in something good. As people discuss the reasons for their conflict, more understanding and appreciation for each other can develop. New creative approaches can be identified as people share their differing perspectives and ideas.

The Bible says, "As iron sharpens iron, so a man sharpens the countenance of his friend" (Prov. 27:17).

Iron sharpens iron through conflict—iron pieces grate against each other to produce a sharp edge. It is through lively, honest, friendly debate, discussion, and argument that our opinions are honed, our thinking becomes clear, and we become more aware of our own beliefs. Friends challenge friends to grow in faith, to be bolder in their witness, and to pursue excellence. — Charles F. Stanley, *Walking Wisely: Real Guidance for Life's Journey* (Nashville, TN: Thomas Nelson Publishers, 2002), 208–209.

19. What is your goal when conflict comes your way? What should our goal be?

Our goal as Christians should always be to bring healing and peaceful resolution in times of conflict. We are to be peacemakers. This is true not only for conflicts that arise between believers, but also for conflicts that erupt between a believer and a nonbeliever. It is up to the Christian to take the lead in seeking a peaceful resolution to a disagreement. The nonbeliever has neither an understanding of genuine inner peace nor motivation to work for peaceful resolution.

If you approach conflict as an opportunity to fight for your cause, to gain vengeance, or to make a statement of self-justification, you are likely to increase the conflict, not decrease it.

When conflict erupts, ask immediately for the Lord to give you an attitude of humility and to help you make peace your goal. — Charles F. Stanley, *Walking Wisely: Real Guidance for Life's Journey* (Nashville, TN: Thomas Nelson Publishers, 2002), 209–210.

20. How do you tend to respond, emotionally, to conflict?

Be realistic about how conflict affects you. The apostle Paul no doubt was sorrowful and discouraged when he learned that people would preach the gospel with a wrong motive (Phil. 1:15–17). Even so, Paul refused to wallow in self-pity or engage in an argument. He chose instead to see the big picture—the result was that the gospel was being preached. He rejoiced in that! In fact, he made rejoicing a conscious decision. Paul wrote, "I rejoice, yes, and will rejoice" (Phil. 1:18). Regardless of how he may have felt personally, he chose to maintain an attitude of contentment, gratitude, and joy.

Be realistic about how you habitually tend to respond to conflict. Some people routinely respond to conflict in very unhealthy ways:

- They suppress their feelings. They deny the impact the conflict is having on them. They stuff all emotions they feel—they deny them or dismiss them completely.

- They repress their feelings. They acknowledge the conflict and their feelings, but they refuse to express their feelings or opinion. Rather, they keep quiet in the hope that the conflict will dissipate, and they can avoid an open confrontation or discussion.

- They are quick to blame and accuse in retaliation. They refuse to accept any part in the conflict.

The person who makes these responses is usually very insecure. He does not want a genuine resolution of a conflict, only a quick fix that causes the immediate pain of the moment to cease.

The problem with all of these approaches is that they produce no clear-cut end to the conflict. Those who repress and suppress their emotions only put their feelings on hold. Feelings that are stifled do not dissipate naturally. Rather, they simmer, soak, ferment, and grow inside a person, and one day they will explode or manifest themselves in sickness. Bitterness and resentment are likely. And the end result of bitterness and resentment is anything but positive: the loss of precious relationships, a loss of joy, a stunting of spiritual growth, and a growing ineffectiveness in one's ability to minister to others.

Check your own response to conflict. If you are dealing with conflict and criticism in a negative way, change your approach! — Charles F. Stanley, *Walking Wisely: Real Guidance for Life's Journey* (Nashville, TN: Thomas Nelson Publishers, 2002), 210–211.

21. Summary. How does the Bible teach us to respond to conflict?

There are at least ten things you can do to create a positive response to a conflict and set the stage for peaceful resolution. These are all things you can do individually and personally, without any participation from the other person in the conflict:

1. Refuse to respond in anger. Choose to adopt and maintain a quiet spirit. No matter what another person says or does, refuse to throw a fit or erupt in frustration. If you have a "short fuse," get a longer one!

2. Make no attempt to defend yourself immediately. Let all the criticism and furor blow over. There may be a time later in which you need to state your case, but until that time comes, keep quiet. When the time for your defense comes, ask the Holy Spirit to tell you what to say. Jesus promised His disciples, "The Holy Spirit will teach you in that very hour what you ought to say" (Luke 12:12).

3. Ask the Holy Spirit to put a seal on your lips and to put a guard on your mouth. Make your prayer in a time of conflict the prayer that David prayed:

> Set a guard, O LORD, over my mouth;
> Keep watch over the door of my lips. (Ps. 141:3)

4. If after calm reflection you still find yourself totally puzzled as to what created a conflict, ask the Holy Spirit to reveal to you the cause. One of the gifts that the Holy Spirit generously bestows on those who request it is discernment. The Holy Spirit does not want you to wander about in confusion—He wants you to know all you need to know to respond to a situation with love, joy, peace, patience, kindness, mercy, and self-control.

5. Regardless of how a conflict arises, see the conflict as coming from God. I'm not saying that the Lord sent or caused the conflict, but He allowed it. And therefore, it comes from Him for a purpose in your life. That purpose is ultimately for your good—for your refinement, strengthening, preparation, and learning. If you see a conflict as having a godly purpose, you are going to be far less likely to lash out at the other person. Rather, you are going to be more willing to forgive, slower to react, and more willing to make changes in your own attitudes and behavior.

6. Ask the Holy Spirit, "Is this my fault?" Ask the Holy Spirit to reveal very specifically any part that you played in bringing about the conflict. If He shows you something that you did to cause or enlarge the conflict, don't run from your responsibility. Admit your fault; ask for forgiveness; make a commitment to change your conduct. Say to the other person, "Is there something you can suggest to me to help me avoid creating a conflict like this in the future?" Give the person an opportunity to vent fully. And as he does, listen closely. There may be a nugget of valuable help in what he says to help you become a more godly person.

7. Forgive the other person. No matter what has happened or what has been said, forgive. We do not have the right as Christians to harbor unforgiveness.

I have heard people say on occasion, "Well, there are some things that just can't be forgiven." Like what? What is it that Jesus couldn't forgive in your life? What is it that Jesus says is beyond His ability to cleanse, heal, restore, or forgive in a person? Take another look at your own past. If God has forgiven you … He expects you to be able to forgive yourself. If God has forgiven you … He expects you to extend that forgiveness to others. Jesus said,

> Therefore be merciful, just as your Father also is merciful. Judge not, and you shall not be judged. Condemn not, and you shall not be condemned. Forgive, and you will be forgiven. (Luke 6:36–37)

Forgiveness does not mean denying that you were hurt or that the matter was important. Rather, forgiveness means letting go and letting God. It means turning another person over to God's judgment. It means trusting God to deal with a person as God chooses, without putting yourself in the way.

It doesn't make any difference if the other person asks for forgiveness or not. Forgive. Your forgiveness should not be withheld pending the other's repentance.

Forgive quickly. The sooner you forgive, the sooner you can receive God's healing for any pain or sorrow you have experienced. God's Word tells us,

> Let all bitterness, wrath, anger, clamor, and evil speaking be put away from you, with all malice. And be kind to one another, tenderhearted, forgiving one another, even as God in Christ forgave you. (Eph. 4:31–32)

8. Begin immediately to treat the other person with genuine kindness and tenderness. Look for a way that you can express love to the other person. Speak well of the person. Find a way to help the person. Pray for the person.

9. Choose to learn something from the conflict. Ask the Holy Spirit, "How can I avoid a conflict such as this in the future?" Ask God to reveal to you the lessons He desires for you to learn and the changes He desires for you to make.

10. View the conflict as an opportunity to respond as Christ would respond. Ask the Holy Spirit to minister through you to the other person. Those who respond to a conflict in a godly manner are strong witnesses for the Lord. You never know who is observing your behavior in a time of criticism or conflict. When you respond without hatred, malice, anger, or bitterness, you send a powerful message about the life-transforming power of God's love and forgiveness. — Charles F. Stanley, *Walking Wisely: Real Guidance for Life's Journey* (Nashville, TN: Thomas Nelson Publishers, 2002), 214–218.

22. How can we support one another in prayer this week?

Joshua, Lesson #6
Good Questions Have Small Groups Talking
www.joshhunt.com

Joshua 24.14 - 26

OPEN

Let's each share your name and one thing you are grateful for.

DIG

1. Verse 14. Should we be afraid of God? What does it mean to fear the Lord?

What does the phrase "fear the Lord" mean? Are we expected to cower with fright in God's presence or live in continual terror and dread?

Fear in this sense is the appropriate response of rebellious unbelievers who flaunt God's decrees. Having rejected Almighty God as a merciful Savior, they now face the grim prospect of meeting him only in his role as the holy Judge of the universe. One the other hand, for the beloved children of God—those whose sins have been forgiven by Christ—"fear the Lord" has a different connotation. The idea for believers is that of awe or stunned admiration in the presence of a great and good Creator. The implication is submissive reverence before a loving Lord, to worship God above all other things. It involves, in the words of the passage, the commitment to "seek" him.

Notice that the promise to those who fear the Lord is that all their needs will be met. Or, as God puts it in another place, "Those who honor me I will honor" (1 Samuel 2:30).

— Livingstone Corporation, *Once-a-Day Bible Promises Devotional* (Grand Rapids, MI: Zondervan, 2012).

2. What difference does it make in our lives when we fear the Lord?

In July of 1861, in an act declaring September 26 as a National Day of Prayer and Fasting, Abraham Lincoln wrote: "It is fit and becoming in all people, at all times, to acknowledge and revere the Supreme Government of God; to bow in humble submission to his chastisement; to confess and deplore their sins and transgressions in the full conviction that the fear of the Lord is the beginning of wisdom..."

That may be one of the best summaries of what it means to "fear the Lord" ever penned. Note the action words: "to acknowledge ... revere ... bow ... confess and deplore." To fear the Lord means more than just one thing. Indeed, it is a phrase that gathers together a number of attitudes and actions. In short, when we fear the Lord, we recognize God's proper place as Creator over us as His creation. If someone followed us around for a week, what evidence would they see that we fear the Lord? Which would they hear most—grumbles or gratitude, complaints or compassion?

A nation that fears the Lord is one whose citizens fear the Lord. Plan a "Personal Day of Prayer and Fasting" soon—a day to reaffirm your own fear of the Lord. — David Jeremiah, *Sanctuary: Finding Moments of Refuge in the Presence of God* (Nashville, TN: Integrity Publishers, 2002), 66.

3. What good things happen to those who fear the Lord?

What does it mean to fear the Lord? It means to be in reverential awe of Him. It means we don't tempt Him. We don't jest with Him. We don't try to make Him do things He will not do. The Israelites did not fear the Lord. They tempted Him. They played with His law and tried to see how close they could get to the world. So God had to discipline them.

God blesses us in three areas of our life when we truly fear Him. First, He will bless us in our walk. "Blessed is every one who fears the LORD, who walks in His ways" (v. 1). This means that our conduct and our character become holy.

Second, God blesses us in our work. "When you eat the labor of your hands, you shall be happy, and it shall be well with you" (v. 2). Some people are unhappy in their work. But if we are obedient to God, we are doing His work no matter what our occupation is and therefore can rejoice in it. When we fear the Lord, we can go to work and be happy.

Third, God blesses us in our homes. "Your wife shall be like a fruitful vine in the very heart of your house, your children like olive plants all around your table" (v. 3). This does not mean that everybody is going to have a family, let alone a big family. It does mean that you'll be a blessing to your family. "Behold, thus shall the man be blessed who fears the LORD" (v. 4). — Warren W. Wiersbe, *Prayer, Praise & Promises: A Daily Walk through the Psalms* (Grand Rapids, MI: Baker Books, 2011), 334.

4. Verse 14. What good things come our way when we serve God?

My own research reveals a strong correlation between happiness and serving. Here was the statement: "I regularly serve God in the way God gifted me to serve." 29% of those who strongly agreed with that statement reported the highest level of happiness. Of those who merely agreed, only 10% were in the happiest group. I couldn't find anyone who was extremely happy who was not serving. None.

The key phrase—I think you would agree—is, "near the sweet spot of the way God gifted you to serve." "Near" suggests that you will never get it perfect. We make two mistakes regarding gifts. One is to ignore the concept altogether and just serve willy-nilly. The other is to be so dedicated to serving according to our gifting that we refuse to do anything else. We should never use the concept of gifts as a cover for laziness. Sometimes, the dishes just need to be done. Still, as much as possible, we should lean into our calling. Leaning into your calling is where FLOW is found.

There is an old story of three men working at laying bricks. Each was asked what he was doing. The first said, "Laying bricks."

The second said, "Feeding my family."

The third said, "I am building a cathedral that will stand a thousand years."

Who do you think is happier?

5. Should we serve God because good things will come our way if we do?

This raises an interesting question. Do we serve God to give or to get? Do we serve God so that God's kingdom will benefit, or do we serve God for what we will get out of it? It certainly sounds more spiritual to say we serve God to give. That is what is popularly taught. I ran across this line in a commentary today: "we cannot follow Christ just for the benefits."

I have seen this kind of sentiment quite a bit over the years— in commentaries, in popular books, in sermons, and in conversations. But, the question is, what does the Bible say?

My favorite verse in the whole Bible: "And without faith it is impossible to please God, because anyone who comes to him must believe that he exists and that he rewards those who earnestly seek him." Hebrews 11:6 (NIV)

We cannot draw near to God except that we believe that God rewards. We must come to him for reward or we cannot come to him. And, if you think about it, it just makes sense. He is rich; I am poor. He has; I lack. He is strong; I am weak. I don't have anything he needs. He is everything I need. I must come to him for my benefit.

John Piper agrees:

You cannot please God if you do not come to Him for reward! Therefore, worship that pleases God is the hedonistic pursuit of God. He is our exceedingly great reward! In His presence is fullness of joy, and at His right hand are pleasures forevermore. Being satisfied with all God is for us in Jesus is the essence of the authentic experience of worship. Worship is the feast of Christian Hedonism.

This raises a question: what about all those verses that speak of commitment? That is the subject of the next chapter. — Josh Hunt, *People Who Enjoy Their God*, 2012.

6. Verse 15. What do we learn about Christian living from this classic verse?

Will is the whole man active. I cannot give up my will, I must exercise it. I must will to obey, and I must will to receive God's Spirit. When God gives a vision of truth it is never a question of what He will do, but of what we will do. The Lord has been putting before us all some big propositions, and the best thing to do is to remember what you did when you were touched by God before—the time when you were saved, or first saw Jesus, or realized some truth. It was easy then to yield allegiance to God; recall those moments now as the Spirit of God brings before you some new proposition.

"Choose you this day whom ye will serve." It is a deliberate calculation, not something into which you drift easily; and everything else is in abeyance until you decide. The proposition is between you and God; do not confer with flesh and blood about it. With every new proposition other people get more and more "out of it," that is where the strain comes. God allows the opinion of His saints to matter to you, and yet you are brought more and more out of the certainty that others understand the step you are taking. You have no business to find out where God is leading, the only thing God will explain to you is Himself.

Profess to Him—"I will be loyal." Immediately you choose to be loyal to Jesus Christ, you are a witness against yourself. Don't consult other Christians but profess before Him—I will serve Thee. I will to be loyal—and give other people credit for being loyal too. — *My Utmost for His Highest.*

7. If God is sovereign, how can man have free will?

The matter of man's free will versus God's sovereignty can be explained in this way: God's sovereignty means that He is in control of everything, that He planned everything from the beginning. Man's free will means that he can, anytime he wants, make most any choice he pleases (within his human limitations, of course). Man's free will can apparently defy the purposes of God and will against the will of God. Now how do we resolve this seeming contradiction?...

Here is what I see: God Almighty is sovereign, free to do as He pleases. Among the things He is pleased to do is give me freedom to do what I please. And when I do what I please, I am fulfilling the will of God, not controverting it, for God in His sovereignty has sovereignly given me freedom to make a free choice.

Even if the choice I make is not the one God would have made for me, His sovereignty is fulfilled in my making the choice. And I can make the choice because the great sovereign God, who is completely free, said to me, "In my sovereign freedom I bestow a little bit of freedom on you. Now 'choose you this day whom ye will serve' (Joshua 24:15)." — *Tozer on the Almighty God: A 366-Day Devotional.*

8. How is Joshua different from many church-goers today?

The word mediocre comes from two Latin words and literally means "halfway to the peak." This makes it an apt description of the progress of many Christians. They are halfway up to the peak....They are morally above the hardened sinner but they are spiritually beneath the shining saint....

Do we really think that this halfway Christian life is the best that Christ offers—the best that we can know? In the face of what Christ offers us, how can we settle for so little? Think of all that He offers us by His blood and by His Spirit, by His sacrificial death on the cross, by His resurrection from the dead, by His ascension to the right hand of the Father, by His sending forth of the Holy Ghost! — *Tozer on the Holy Spirit.*

9. It is always a good idea to read the Bible for emotion. What is Joshua feeling in this verse?

It is the spark of God within a person that troubles him or her. That spark is placed within by the Spirit of God. Conviction. Longing. Desire. That spark within does not save. But that spark must be there to lead the person on to salvation.

Why is it that some men and women seem never to have any awareness of that spark from God? They may be nice people, nice neighbors, nice friends. But they live every day without any spark of discontent, without any spark of need for God....

God has made us with the right to make our own choices. We were not created to be robots. God made us in His own image, but with the right and the ability to choose. We are free moral agents.

When our first parents made the wrong choices, the human race became alienated from God. Since that time, every person has been faced with choices and decisions. — *Tozer on the Holy Spirit.*

10. What are the people feeling as they respond?

Notice that they referred to the Lord as "the Lord our God." Notice also that they pledged not to forsake Him because He "did those great signs in our sight."

This first generation of Promised Land people were highly committed to God because they had personally seen Him do great things as He delivered them from Egypt and preserved them in the wilderness. As children, they had witnessed the tenplagues and the parting of the Dead Sea. They had tasted with their own mouths the manna from heaven. They had seen the pillar of cloud guiding them by day and the pillar of fire at night. They had crossed into the Promised Land on dry land as they saw God miraculously part the Jordan River.

They had marched around Jericho for seven days and had seen God knock down the massive walls of the city. They had a personal commitment to God based on a personal relationship with God because of their personal experience with God.

Not only was this generation the first generation to inhabit the Promised Land, but they were also the first generation to experience God's miraculous work in delivering His people from Egypt. First-generation followers of God tend be highly committed to Him because of the wonders He has done in their lives. — Dave Earley, *14 Secrets to Better Parenting: Powerful Principles from the Bible* (Uhrichsville, OH: Barbour, 2011).

11. Joshua does not seem to believe them. Why do you think this is?

Immediately the people answered that they stood in unanimous agreement with Joshua and would never serve other gods. They reviewed God's leadership in their nation and blessing upon their lives and loudly proclaimed, We too will serve the Lord, because he is our God.

But the verses which follow seem to suggest that they were unable to convince Joshua by this great acclamation. What they said should have pleased him. But it seems as if Joshua were stopping them as they rushed to the altar to make their commitment and sending them back to rethink it. He appears to say, "You don't know what you're committing to. You're not serious enough about this. You don't realize how holy God is and that he won't just ignore your sin and idolatry. You haven't yet counted the cost of serving God." He actually told them that this jealous God... will not forgive your rebellion and your sins, a point we will return to in "Deeper Discoveries." But they persisted and repeatedly said, We will serve the Lord. They were willing to be witnesses against themselves to this covenant commitment. — *Holman Old Testament Commentary – Joshua.*

12. Verse 26. What was the purpose of this stone? What is the lesson for us?

We need stones with ears in our lives. We need reminders of who we are and whose we are. When I see my wife's picture, I am reminded of my commitment to her. When I see my ordination certificate, I am reminded of my commitment to ministry. When I see the American flag, I remember my commitment to my country. And when I sign my income tax forms, I remember my commitment to the laws and financial statutes of our nation.

Stones with ears. Visual reminders of our commitments to God, his word, his work, his people. Perhaps in a picture or even a bookmark. Maybe a poster or plaque on the wall. Maybe a special letter in a purse or wallet. We need stones with ears to remind us of our commitments to God as well as his commitments to us. — *Holman Old Testament Commentary – Joshua.*

13. How did this work out for them? Were they obedient? What is the lesson for us?

Resolve alone will not do. We need God living inside us through the power of the Holy Spirit. "To this end I labor, struggling with all his energy, which so powerfully works in me." Colossians 1:29 (NIV) We need to walk with a profound awareness that we cannot live the Christian life unless He lives His life through us. There is more to Christian living that trying hard to be good. Much more.

14. We are not tempted to serve idols, right? What is the application for us?

"As for me and my house, we will serve the Lord," Joshua declared with certainty.

"We want to serve the Lord, too," the people said.

"You can't," Joshua said.

Why? Because he knew it was "idle" talk. As we shall see, Joshua knew the people had idols in their tents and in their homes. He knew they were talking the talk but not prepared to walk the walk. He knew they would say, "Hip, hip, hooray for the Lord" in the midst of the congregation. But in reality, their idols would be at home waiting for them.

The Israelites had already begun to worship idols—the multi-breasted Ashteroth that spoke of sensuality, Baal that spoke of the intellect, Mammon that spoke of money. They had already begun to collect these idols—symbols of hedonism, intellectualism, materialism. Joshua knew this.

Concerning idols, the Lord said to Ezekiel,

> Son of man, these men have set up their idols in their heart, and put the stumblingblock of their iniquity before their face: should I be inquired of at all by them? Therefore speak unto them, and say unto them, Thus saith the Lord GOD; Every man of the house of Israel that setteth up his idols in his heart, and putteth the stumblingblock of his iniquity before his face, and cometh to the prophet; I the LORD will answer him that cometh according to the multitude of his idols.   Ezekiel 14:3, 4

I've often been baffled by people who say, "God has given me peace about having an affair," or, "I've prayed about leaving my husband," or, "I have peace about having this cable channel in my house." How could it be that a person could look us in the eye and say, "God has told me..." something that is exactly contrary to the Word? Ezekiel says if there's an idol in your heart and you seek the Lord, you'll hear the voice of your idol and think it's the voice of God.

Stay away from idols, gang. I'm not talking about statues. I'm talking about passions, compromises, flirting with stuff you know is not right. They will lie to you and tell you you're in God's will. But you'll be deceived, disgraced, and carried away captive into a foreign country—into a place or a situation in which you don't want to be—just like the Israelites would be. — Jon Courson, *Jon Courson's Application Commentary:*

Volume One: Genesis–Job (Nashville, TN: Thomas Nelson, 2005), 705–706.

15. Why does idolatry have such a pull? What is the attraction?

If we think of idolatry as referring only to worshipping pagan gods, we've missed an important bit of truth in our own walk with God. Ezekiel wrote that the people of Israel were "taking their idols into their hearts" (see Ezekiel 14:4). Idolatry is a matter of mental images that we cling to, whether the aspirations of the flesh, or preoccupation with our own selfish ambition. To put it clearly, idolatry is nothing more than valuing something else more than we do God and our relationship to Him.

Joshua asked that the people of Israel put their idols behind them. In their case, that meant smashing the physical idols that they had brought with them out of Egypt. We should not be surprised that the people had brought their "gods" with them from Egypt, for false deities are actually empowered by demonic forces, and for this reason it's difficult to break these occult attachments. Witness, for example, the difficulty some people in Japan have had in breaking away from the tradition of worshipping their ancestors, or a Catholic's inordinate preoccupation with a crucifix. Humans find it difficult to break attachments to physical objects, but mental idolatry is just as captivating and addictive.

This week we will pray about smashing our idols, specifically habitual sins or addictions that hold us captive to our own lusts and desires. Whether it is possessions, personal pursuits, achievements, sexual addictions, or alcohol or drugs, these kinds of obsessions and sins and others like them have great power over the human will. Human determination, though laudable, simply cannot break these bondages.

Here are a few lines I memorized some time ago from William Cowper's hymn "O for a Closer Walk with God":

> The dearest idol I have known,
> Whate'er that idol be

Help me to tear it from Thy throne,
And worship only Thee.

—Erwin Lutzer, *Covering Your Life in Prayer: Discover a Life-Changing Conversation with God* (Eugene, OR: Harvest House, 2013).

16. What do we learn about God from today's passage?

Have you ever had one of those indecisive days? I am usually decisive. But I get in those moods where I just can't decide. I can be at the window of a take-out place and suddenly be stricken with indecision. That's not so tragic at a take-out window. But when people are indecisive with God, it is a serious problem.

That's how it was with Israel in Elijah's day. For 85 years, the nation had gone back and forth between false gods and the true God. Not wanting to be responsible or live under absolutes, they would follow some other god. Then they would reap the results of following that god and would scurry back to the Lord and say they were sorry until their problems went away. Then they would go back like wayward children and do the same thing again. Every time they were on the brink of destruction, God would be merciful and forgive them. One day, Elijah basically said to them, "Enough is enough. Make a choice. Which side are you on?"

Moses posed a similar question to Israel when they fell before the golden calf. He said, "Whoever is on the Lord's side—come to me!" (Exodus 32:26). His successor Joshua challenged Israel to "Choose for yourselves this day whom you will serve ..." (Joshua 24:15). And in Matthew 12:30 Jesus said, "He who is not with Me is against Me, and he who does not gather with Me scatters abroad." Jesus demands a response. He demands us to decide which side we're on. Choose this day whom you will serve. — Greg Laurie, *For Every Season: Daily Devotions* (Dana Point, CA: Kerygma Publishing—Allen David Books, 2011).

17. What do we learn about Christian living?

When we come to the message of the gospel, we must say yes or no to it. Either we are in or we are out. Either we are for or we are against Jesus Christ. Moses told the people of Israel, "I call heaven and earth as witnesses today against you, that I have set before you life and death, blessing and cursing; therefore choose life …" (Deuteronomy 30:19).

After Joshua led Israel into the Promised Land, he confronted them with a choice: " 'Choose for yourselves this day whom you will serve. … But as for me and my house, we will serve the Lord' " (Joshua 24:15).

On Mt. Carmel, Elijah challenged the people with the same choice and said, " 'How long will you falter between two opinions? If the Lord is God, follow Him; but if Baal, follow him' " (1 Kings 18:21).

We, too, must make a choice.

Narrow is the way that leads to life. Christianity is not the most popular way to live. If you truly follow Jesus Christ, then you will be a part of a minority. And in case you haven't noticed, it is open season on followers of Jesus. We have seen Christians ridiculed. We have seen Christianity exaggerated. We have seen our message distorted. If you truly follow Jesus Christ, then you will have some difficulties in life.

Although it is true that it costs to follow Jesus, it is also true that it costs a whole lot more not to follow Him. Whatever it costs to follow Jesus Christ, it is worth it. And whatever you give up, He will make up to you. — Greg Laurie, *For Every Season: Daily Devotions* (Dana Point, CA: Kerygma Publishing—Allen David Books, 2011).

18. Why couldn't they serve God AND serve these other gods? What is the lesson for us?

The people were nominally serving Yahweh, but in reality they served other gods too. They were to serve God 'in sincerity' (no hypocrisy), 'and in truth' (honestly and with integrity). There was to be separation from all false gods. The choice was to be immediate—'this day'. 'Today' they must choose!

This confrontation must have been a mighty shock! Suddenly it was in their face! When people are confronted with God's terms they sometimes blame the preacher for being so personal when they should rather seek the Lord! The summons of Joshua speaks as loudly today as it did then.

The gods he mentions here are, firstly, those beyond the River, that is the Euphrates: the gods that Abraham served when he dwelt in Ur of the Chaldees, the Babylonian gods. Amazingly they had maintained this allegiance! Secondly, he speaks of the gods of Egypt. They are the gods of the Nile, the sun, the land and the sky. Thirdly, he speaks of the gods of the Amorites, in whose land they dwell. These were gods which demanded the sacrifice of their children, and which were served with cultic prostitution. They were dreadful and immoral gods.

The clear demand was to serve the Lord. If they served the Lord they would have to get rid of their other gods which they were worshipping. They were to choose to serve the Lord intelligently, decisively and willingly. If that was unacceptable, their choice was not between the Lord and the other gods, it was between the different sets of gods! They were called upon to choose to serve the gods of Babylon or the gods of the Amorites. 'That is your choice—choose,' said Joshua. Joshua was using shock treatment. This was exclusion! This was radical stuff! Was Joshua forbidding them from worshipping the Lord? 'No! No! Joshua, what are you saying to us?' — Colin N. Peckham, *Joshua: A Devotional Commentary, Exploring the Bible Commentary* (Leominster, UK: Day One Publications, 2007), 228–229.

19. What do you want to recall from today's discussion?

In the 1700s, a young man named James Taylor proposed marriage to his girlfriend, and a wedding date was set. Neither of them were Christians. James, in fact, so detested itinerant preachers that he often pelted them with rotten tomatoes or eggs.

Shortly before his wedding, one of John Wesley's circuit riders entered town, and James, hearing of it, wanted to disrupt the meeting. But as James listened in the fringes of the crowd, the preacher quoted Joshua 24:15: But as for me and my house, we will serve the Lord.

The words stuck James like an arrow.

When the day of his wedding arrived, the verse was still lodged in his thoughts. That morning James retired to the fields to think. He was about to take a wife, to establish a home, but he wasn't serving the Lord. He knelt in the grass and earnestly asked Christ to be his Savior. By the time he finished praying, he was alarmed to discover it was time for the wedding.

Rushing to the chapel, he apologized for being late, and the ceremony proceeded. Then he shocked his bride and guests, by announcing he had become a Christian. He soon began witnessing to his new wife, but she remained resistant. Finally one day James came home so burdened for her that he picked her up and carried her to the bedroom. There with a forceful hand he made her kneel beside him. Soon both were weeping, and there she, too, became a Christian.

Eight generations have since passed, each filled with Christian workers serving the Lord. Included among them is James Taylor's great-grandson, Hudson Taylor, founder of the China Inland Mission, who opened the interior of China to the gospel of Jesus Christ. — Robert J. Morgan, *From This Verse: 365 Scriptures That Changed the World, electronic ed.* (Nashville: Thomas Nelson Publishers, 2000).

20. How can we support one another in prayer this week?

1. "You can do more than pray after you have prayed; but you can never do more than pray until you have prayed." A.J. Gordon

2. "God does nothing except in response to believing prayer." John Wesley (Famous evangelist who spent 2 hours daily in prayer)

3. "Prayer strikes the winning blow; service is simply picking up the pieces." S.D. Gordon

4. "One should never initiate anything that he cannot saturate with prayer."

5. "The greatest thing anyone can do for God or man is pray." S.D. Gordon

6. "If I fail to spend two hours in prayer each morning, the devil gets the victory through the day. I have so much business I cannot get on without spending three hours daily in prayer. Martin Luther

7. "The most important thing a born again Christian can do is to pray." Chuck Smith

8. "Prayer doesn't change the purpose of God, but prayer can change the action of God." Chuck Smith (Note: S.D. Gordon penned a similar quote).

9. "Men may spurn our appeals, reject our message, oppose our arguments, despise our persons, but they are helpless against our prayers." Sidlow Baxter

10. "God shapes the world by prayer. The more prayer there is in the world the better the world will be, the mightier the forces of against evil ..." E.M. Bounds

11. "Prayer is where the action is." John Wesley

12. "Satan does not care how many people read about prayer if only he can keep them from praying. Paul E. Billheimer http://www.christian-prayer-quotes.christian-attorney.net/

Made in the USA
Monee, IL
09 August 2022

11186739R00056